thai *cooking*

ai cooking

Jackum Brown

consultant: Rachanee Boonthon

photography by Sandra Lane

hamlyn

Publishing Director: Laura Bamford

Editor: Anne Crane
Assistant Editor: Sharyn Conlan
Creative Director: Keith Martin
Senior Designer: Geoff Fennel
Photographer: Sandra Lane
Home Economist: Oona Van den Berg
Stylist: Mary Norden
Indexer: Hilary Bird
Production Controller: Bonnie Ashby

Thai Cooking
Jackum Brown

First published in Great Britain in 1998 by Hamlyn
a division of Octopus Publishing Group Limited
2–4 Heron Quays, London E14 4JP

This paperback edition first published in 2002

Copyright © 1996, 2002 Octopus Publishing Group
Limited

British Library Cataloguing-in-Publication Data
A catalogue record for this book is available from
the British Library

ISBN 0 600 60715 1

Produced by Toppan
Printed in China

Author's acknowledgements

I owe a great many thanks to Rachanee Boonthon for helping me create these
recipes, and for spending countless afternoons with me in her restaurant, the Thai
Cafe in Fortess Road, London NW5; Benjarmas and Kitisak Boonthon were also
very helpful. Thanks are due to David Brown, Gabrielle Mander, Nigel Fountain and
Monica Henriquez, without whom I could not possibly have managed.

Notes

All dishes serve 4 people, when served as part of a Thai meal.

Standard level spoon measurements are used in all recipes.
1 tablespoon = one 15 ml spoon
1 teaspoon = one 5 ml spoon

Both imperial and metric measurements have been given in all recipes. Use one set of measurements only and not a mixture of both.

Eggs should be medium (size 3) unless otherwise stated.

Milk should be full fat unless otherwise stated.

Pepper should be freshly ground black pepper unless otherwise stated.

Fresh herbs should be used unless otherwise stated. If unavailable use dried herbs as an alternative but halve the quantities stated.

Ovens should be preheated to the specified temperature – if using a fan assisted oven, follow the manufacturer's instructions for adjusting the time and temperature.

Thai cooks rarely deseed chillies (the seeds and surrounding membrane are the hottest part). If you prefer a milder flavour, remove the seeds before use.

contents

Thailand is a beautiful and fertile country which produces some of the best food in the world. There is no doubting the importance of good food to Thai people – from the moment you set foot in the country your senses are assailed from all sides with the smell of delicious barbecue chicken and dried squid, the sound of pestles thudding into mortars, cleavers chopping vegetables and the sight of exotic fruits loaded on to stalls, whilst out of the corner of your eye you see a huge whoosh of flame reaching up around a wok and the cook laughing at your surprise.

Food markets in Thailand are an absolute joy to explore: the produce is so fresh and so exotic to look at and there are always scores of mysterious items for sale which you have never seen before. Thailand is still overwhelmingly an agricultural country and its major natural resource is its agricultural potential. Although the agricultural sector's contribution to Thailand's GNP has declined considerably in the last 40 years due to the huge growth in manufacturing output, it still employs two-thirds of the labour force and directly supports sixty per cent of the population.

Introduction

Thailand is one of the only countries in Asia to export more food than it imports, and has been the world's largest exporter of rice since 1981. Most Thai rice is produced under natural rain-fed conditions, using little fertiliser, so production depends on prevailing weather conditions. As the world's weather patterns become more and more erratic, the late or non-appearance of monsoons or the extreme conditions of drought, flooding and hurricanes as produced by El Niño, for example, may prove disastrous for all of us and not just for the citizens of the countries that are directly affected.

The good thing about countries like Thailand, where the agriculture is still largely unintensive, is the fabulous quality of what is produced. Problems arise where intensive farming for profit is undertaken too hurriedly. For example, in Thailand cassava (tapioca), which is a subsistence crop in most countries that grow it, is almost all exported to Europe, mainly as cattle food pellets. However, production is declining as it makes heavy demands on soil nutrients, and soil erosion and exhaustion are being reported. Similarly, overfishing has depleted in-shore fish stocks, though aquaculture and the development of canning and freezing facilities have greatly expanded the export of shrimp, prawn and squid to Japan, the USA and Europe.

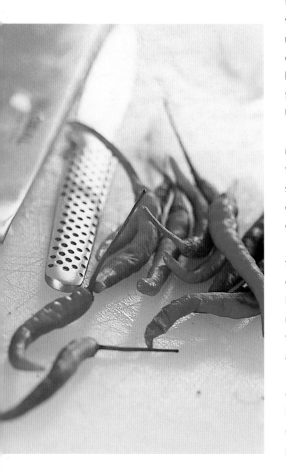

The Thai diet is a very healthy one – plenty of fresh vegetables and fruit, good quality rice, noodles and small amounts of meat and fish. Dairy products are virtually unused by the majority of Thai people and cattle raising is on a small scale. In fact there has been something of a beef shortage over the last decade, forcing a steep rise in beef imports. The climate and topography of Thailand are not very suitable for cattle – you find far more pigs, chickens and ducks and this is reflected in the recipes.

There are about 60 million people living in Thailand, the vast majority of whom are of the Thai ethnic group and are Therevada Buddhists. Buddhism was adopted in the 13th century and Buddhist teaching has given rise to a reluctance to take the life of any creature. Historically, wealthy Thais would try to gain merit by buying a whole catch of fish and returning it to the sea. Nowadays you can buy little songbirds in bamboo cages and set them free for the same purpose. Butchers are rarely ethnic Thais though fishermen are another matter.

Fish is very important in the Thai diet and always has been. The whole country is crossed by rivers and natural waterways, so freshwater fish and shellfish are readily available in places where fresh fish from the sea is unobtainable. Much fish of all types is dried, salted or turned into fish paste or fish sauce – all highly nutritious and essential providers of protein. If you ask how fishing – a very popular activity – squares with Buddhism, you will

Left: chillies; Above: stir-frying noodles; Above right: Stir-Fried Squid with Basil (see page 86)

often receive a big smile along with the expression "Mai Pen Rai" (no problem). Ask again and the most essentially Thai explanation is that fish stupidly get caught in traps and have to be rescued from drowning! Fishermen don't kill them, but if they then die, why shouldn't they be eaten?

Thailand's cuisine has been influenced by various different countries and the Thais have refined all these influences to form a unique style of their own – highly spiced with sharply contrasting flavours and textures. There are clean citrus tastes from kaffir limes, lime leaves and lemon grass, and sour tamarind, sweet coconut milk and palm sugar, distinctive ginger, galangal and krachai, essential garlic and all-pervading chillies. Chillies were brought to Thailand in the early 16th century by the Portuguese. Until then, hot black pepper was used, but chillies loved the climate in Thailand and the Thais loved chillies. Cardamom came from India via Burma, coriander and cumin arrived from the Middle East, tapioca from Central America and tomatoes from South America via Europe.

A Thai meal generally consists of a number of different dishes plus a large bowl of rice. There might be a soup – either in a large bowl which everyone can dip into, or small individual bowls – a curry, something steamed or fried, a salad, some noodles, various different sauces and pickles and fresh fruit to finish the meal. All these dishes will appear on the table at the same time and you put a mound of rice on your plate, followed by a little of one of the other dishes. Thais do not put everything on their plates at once and eat it all together. They like to appreciate all the different tastes and textures separately. Thais use either their fingers or a fork and spoon to eat with, except in the case of noodles, where chopsticks are used – a sign of Chinese influence on Thai cuisine.

Unless it is a special occasion you will not find a dessert being served, other than fruit. There are a large number of Thai desserts or sweetmeats, and a great many of them involve egg yolks and sugar – another legacy of the Portuguese. Some of them take a long time to make and involve a number of different stages. I sometimes wonder whether they aren't more highly prized because of the length of time involved in their making rather than for the tastes themselves. Generally speaking, most Thais lead hard, busy lives and do not spend hours cooking complicated food. They go to the market and find whatever looks good that day, take it home and rustle up something delicious in a very short space of time. While we were cooking the recipes that appear in this book, my friend and consultant Rachanee suddenly became quite worried: "Everyone will say, 'Oh, it's too quick, it's too easy, it can't be right'," but that is one of the joys of cooking Thai-style – as long as you have the basic ingredients, you can make a delicious meal quickly and without much trouble.

Thai kitchens are very simple compared to our sophisticated Western kitchens, so you will probably already have most of the equipment you need to cook Thai food. You really do need a wok, though, and I suggest a wooden-handled one; some of the cheaper woks have metal handles and you can give yourself a bad burn if you aren't careful. The shape of the wok allows its entire surface to heat up, with the hottest part at the centre. When you stir-fry it is best to heat the wok, add a little oil, swirl it around and get it good and hot before you add your first ingredients. Think about what you are cooking, and put in the ingredients that require most cooking first, leaving delicate leaves or bean sprouts to the end. Don't be afraid of tossing the food around in the wok; you need to keep moving it from the centre to the sides and back again. The whole experience of Thai cooking is very much hands-on – there is lots of chopping and pounding and tearing and mincing. Most Thais do not have ovens so they have not evolved the sort of long, slow casserole cooking or roasting that we go in for.

You will also need a steamer, ideally either a stainless steel one, which you will find very useful in your everyday cooking too, or a bamboo steamer of the kind you can find in an oriental shop. A mortar and pestle is useful for blending together chillies, garlic, onions and other spices and achieving an authentic texture. A cleaver is a very useful item for peeling and chopping vegetables, chopping through bones and opening pineapples and coconuts. A bamboo-handled wire basket can be used for blanching vegetables, plunging noodles into stock or boiling water for a few moments to cook, and for removing deep-fried food from the hot oil. A long-handled spatula is also useful – shaped rather like a shovel with a long handle, it is ideal for moving the ingredients around whilst stir-frying.

Having said all this though, there are always alternatives. You could use a large frying pan instead of a wok, rig up a colander over a large saucepan of water as a steamer – just put a lid over whatever you are steaming – I always cook rice this way. A slotted spoon can be used for removing deep-fried food from the oil and can also be used for stir-frying – as can wooden spoons. You can use a small food processor or coffee grinder instead of a mortar and pestle, though if you use the coffee grinder for its original purpose, make sure you clean it out thoroughly both before and after whizzing up your spices, or you might find yourself drinking chilli-hot coffee with overtones of lime leaf and coriander!

Thais do eat very, very hot food. Not every dish, of course, contains chillies, but you would never have a Thai meal that wasn't hot in part. Some of the recipes in this book may be too hot for chilli-beginners, so deseed the chillies to tone down the heat. Be very careful when handling them – they contain an oil which is so strong it can even make your skin sting, so wash your hands really thoroughly, scrubbing under the nails, and don't touch your eyes, nose or mouth straight after touching chillies. Generally speaking, the smaller the chilli, the hotter it is; when they are young and green they tend to be hotter than when they are mature and red or yellow. To deseed them you hold the stem in one hand and, with the sharp point of a knife, you split the chilli from top to tip and then scrape out the white

Below: Bamboo steamers; Right: Grilled Beef with Spicy Sauce (see page 62); Far right: Deep-fried Sea Bass (see page 80).

seeds and ribs inside. With dried chillies, just take the stem end off and roll the chilli around in your fingers to loosen the seeds which will then fall out of the open end.

If you are thinking of really getting into cooking Thai food, I would recommend taking a trip to an oriental food store or supermarket. Here you will not only be able to buy everything you need, in both food and equipment terms, but also very economically. Although most supermarkets and many corner shops carry some useful items, such as noodles, bamboo shoots and soy sauce, they cannot compete with the real thing. For example, Thai jasmine or fragrant rice can be bought in 5 or 10 kilo sacks, which will last a long time and is considerably cheaper than buying it in individual boxes or bags of 500 g/1 lb.

Cooking Thai-style may seem a little alarming to begin with – so many small amounts of different things go into each dish, and somehow a number of different dishes have to be ready to eat at more or less the same time. The answer is to choose your menu carefully. Rice can be reheated very easily in a steamer. Curries can also be cooked in advance and reheated. Soup can be cooked in a saucepan, leaving your wok free for deep-frying a fish or stir-frying, and salads can be prepared in advance and finished at the last moment. As with any other form of cooking, the more often you do it the easier it becomes, until you find you can turn out inexpensive, nutritious meals at the drop of a hat and your family and friends will consider you a star. Whether or not you become addicted to Thai food, you will certainly know that you are eating healthily, and I am sure you will enjoy its scented and exotic flavours.

Jackum Brown

Aubergine Asian aubergines are either long and thin and pink, small and round and pale green, or tiny, round and darker green. They are often available in large supermarkets and Asian and oriental food shops. If you substitute the large purple-black variety more commonly found, remember that they cook faster than the Asian varieties, so adjust your cooking times accordingly.

Basil Holy basil is used as commonly as sweet (European) basil in Thai cookery. It has a smaller, darker leaf and purple stalks. It is less sweet than European basil, which may also be substituted.

Bamboo shoots Young, ivory-coloured, conical-shaped shoots of edible bamboo plants. They are tender and slightly crunchy and add texture and sweetness to many Asian dishes. Bamboo shoots are available canned, fresh and sometimes vacuum-packed.

Bean sauce Black, yellow and red bean sauces made from preserved soya beans are available in jars. Black beans are available in cans and bags and should be rinsed and chopped before use. Unused beans and their liquid can be stored indefinitely if they are kept in a sealed container in the refrigerator. Bean sauce and beans can be bought from most supermarkets and oriental food shops.

Chillies There are so many different kinds of chilli that it would be impossible to list them all. As a general rule, the smaller the chilli the fiercer the heat. Red chillies are slightly less fierce than green since they become sweeter as they ripen. Most of the heat of chillies is contained in and around the seeds and the inner membrane. Thai cooks often include the seeds in cooking, but you may prefer to remove them for a milder flavour. Fresh orange and yellow chillies are often used in Thai cooking, for their pretty colours as much as anything else. You can occasionally buy them from specialist oriental shops and markets, but otherwise use whatever colour you can get.

Chinese broccoli This is available fresh at oriental shops. It is quite like European sprouting broccoli except that it is longer and thinner, with more stalk and less floret. The stalk is the most interesting part, and it is sliced and cooked in many different ways.

Coconut milk and cream These are widely available in cans, packets and blocks (which

Glossary

require added water). You can make coconut milk yourself from desiccated coconut: place 175 g/6 oz coconut in a blender with 300 ml/½ pint hand-hot water; blend for 30 seconds then strain the liquid through muslin, squeezing it as dry as you can. This will produce thick coconut milk. If you return the coconut to the blender and repeat the process, then mix the two extractions, you will get a medium-thick coconut milk, suitable for most dishes. If you put this milk in the refrigerator the 'cream' will rise to the surface and can be taken off. Coconut milk only lasts 1–2 days, even in the refrigerator. If you are using coconut cream, stir it all the time while cooking because it curdles easily.

Coriander An essential ingredient in Thai cooking. All of this wonderful herb is used – the leaves, stalks and roots. You can store the roots in an airtight container in the refrigerator or in the freezer.

Curry paste Ready-made pastes are available in jars and packets, or you can make your own (see pages 18–19). They freeze perfectly.

Fish sauce Thais use fish sauce in a great many dishes. It is available in most large supermarkets and in oriental food shops.

Galangal This is a root similar to ginger, but the skin is thinner and slightly pink, and the taste is more mellow. It is available in large supermarkets and oriental food shops. It is peeled before use, then either sliced or chopped according to individual recipes. Sliced or chopped galangal can be kept in an airtight container in the refrigerator for up to 2 weeks; it also

Left: fresh coriander; Below: greater galangal (sometimes called Thai ginger); Right: gai choy (mustard cabbage).

freezes well. Dried slices are also available, and 1 dried slice is the equivalent to 1 cm/½ inch of the fresh root. Powdered galangal can also be found, but it is not as good.

Ginger Fresh root ginger is readily available. Use it as galangal, above.

Garlic White garlic is a main ingredient in Thai cooking and is used in abundance. The size of the clove doesn't really affect the flavour, although very large cloves are milder.

Glutinous rice A variety of short-grain rice used in many Thai desserts. It is sometimes called 'sticky' rice.

Krachai Also called lesser ginger, this root is smaller and fiercer than ginger and galangal, but it comes from the same family and should be treated in the same way. It is sometimes available fresh from oriental food shops or dried in packets.

Laver A type of seaweed which can be found in most large supermarkets, health food shops and oriental food shops.

Lemon grass Available from supermarkets in bundles of 4–6 stalks, the straw-like tops of lemon grass should be trimmed as well as the ends, and the stalks thinly sliced. If you can't get fresh lemon grass, dried and powdered lemon grass is also available, or you can use lemon rind or juice as a substitute.

Limes and lime leaves The variety of lime grown in Thailand is called kaffir. It is slightly different from the ones we normally see, which make a perfectly adequate substitute. Kaffir lime leaves can be bought fresh or dried in oriental food shops and large supermarkets; if unavailable use lime rind or juice, or lemon rind or juice as a last resort.

Mushrooms Many sorts of mushrooms are used in Thai cookery. These are a few:

Dried black fungus (cloud ear mushrooms) can be found in packets in oriental food shops. Soak them in warm water for 15–20 minutes, then drain before use.

Oyster mushrooms are available fresh from most supermarkets.

Shiitake mushrooms can be found dried in oriental food shops, health food shops and some supermarkets, which also sell them fresh occasionally. If dried, they should be soaked in warm water for 15–20 minutes before use, then the hard stalk cut away and added to the stockpot. Shiitake are expensive, but you only need to use a few at a time.

Straw mushrooms can be found in cans from supermarkets.

Button, chestnut and field mushrooms can be used if none of the others is available.

Noodles There are many different kinds of noodles used in Thai cooking, but the most commonly available are egg noodles, rice vermicelli, rice sticks and glass noodles.

Egg noodles can be bought fresh from oriental shops, but the dried ones, which are widely available at supermarkets, are just as good.

Rice vermicelli are very thin, white and transparent-looking, made from rice as their name suggests. They are dried in long bundles, but can easily be cut into more convenient lengths.

Rice sticks are the same as vermicelli, only wider and flatter. They come in varying widths, and it is a matter of personal preference which ones you choose. Occasionally fresh rice sticks (Ho Fun) can be found in oriental shops; these are white and slippery, and can be cut to any desired width. They do not keep well, and so should be used on the day of purchase.

Glass noodles are also known as cellophane noodles, bean thread noodles and bean vermicelli. They are very like rice vermicelli, but made from mung beans rather than rice.

Oil Groundnut oil is ideal, although corn oil or other vegetable oils can be used. Do not use olive oil because the taste is too distinctive. After using oil for deep-frying, let it cool, then strain it through a fine sieve or muslin back into the bottle for future use. If you like, you can then keep this oil specially for Thai cooking.

Oriental greens Thais use many different green vegetables in their cookery including bok choy, choy sum, gai choy, chinese cabbage and chinese leaves. Many are now available from supermarkets and specialist shops: use whichever you can get hold of.

Palm sugar This soft, raw light brown sugar is widely used in south-east Asia. In Thailand it is often sold wet, giving it a thick, honey-like consistency, but it is exported in hard blocks that can be broken into pieces and dissolved. It tastes delicious and has a golden colour that is especially attractive in desserts like coconut custard. If you can't get it, use a light muscovado or Indian jaggery sugar.

Papaya Also called pawpaw, this tropical fruit is available from supermarkets. When unripe, the green flesh is used in salads. The orange flesh of ripe papaya tastes good with lime juice.

Shrimp Paste Available 'fresh' or dried in plastic tubs or wrapped blocks, this is made of salted decomposed shrimp and is rich in Vitamin B. It is a major source of protein in many south-east Asian diets. The dried blocks are stronger than the 'fresh' but they are very strong smelling. Probably only available in oriental food shops.

Spring roll wrappers White and flimsy, these are made from flour and water, and are usually square. Buy them ready-made, fresh or frozen in plastic bags, from oriental shops. They are very fragile, so handle them gently, especially if they have been frozen. If you can't find the shape you need for a recipe, buy whatever you can and cut to the required shape. If spring roll wrappers prove hard to find, use filo pastry instead, and cut the sheets to size.

Tamarind water Dried tamarind pulp can be found in oriental and Indian food shops. Simmer for 2–3 minutes in water, cool, then squeeze out the juice and discard the pulp and seeds. Tamarind concentrate can be bought in tubs – just dissolve a spoonful in hot water. You can substitute lemon juice.

Tofu Made from soya beans, tofu is highly nutritious and absorbs other flavours, making it a versatile addition to a vegetarian diet. There are several kinds of tofu available. One of the

Above: fresh flat egg noodles; Above right: fresh egg noodles; Far right: fresh ginger and krachai.

most useful types is fresh white tofu, which is sold in blocks in its own liquid. It is very delicate and will break up if stirred too much. Silken tofu is even more delicate. It does not keep long. Blocks of ready-fried tofu are golden brown on the outside and much more solid. They are ideal for stir-frying. You can buy fairly solid white tofu cakes packed in water in plastic containers; these can be used for stir-frying if you can't get the ready-fried kind. Sheets of tofu, sometimes called 'bean-curd skins', are made from heated soya milk. They are dried, and need to be soaked for 2–3 hours before use. All of these products are available in health food shops, supermarkets and oriental food shops.

Turmeric This spice is a wonderful colourant with a very mild flavour. Although it can sometimes be found fresh in oriental and Asian food shops, it is most often used in its dried powder form.

Vinegar It is worth looking for white rice vinegar or distilled white vinegar in large supermarkets or oriental shops. If you cannot find them, use cider vinegar. Malt vinegar will not suit oriental food.

Wonton wrappers Made from flour and eggs, these are deep yellow or brown in colour. They are sold ready-made, fresh or frozen in plastic bags, from oriental food shops. If a recipe uses differently shaped wrappers, cut them to shape with scissors. Otherwise, use sheets of filo pastry and cut them to the required shape.

basics

Many of the following basic recipes are for items which you can buy in ready-made versions – the majority of these are absolutely fine. However it is interesting and useful to know how to make them yourself and, in the case of the exotic curry pastes, quite fun too. Of course you can buy all sorts of different Thai curry pastes these days: the best selections are found in oriental food stores. You can use stock cubes for your stock if you are in a rush but don't forget to add some extra spices and herbs to cheer them up. Dried garlic and onion flakes work well if dry-fried.

panang curry paste

- Put all of the ingredients in a blender or food processor and blend to a smooth paste.
- Alternatively, you can pound all the ingredients together with a mortar and pestle.
- Transfer the paste to an airtight container and store in the refrigerator for up to 3 weeks.

4 shallots, chopped

8 garlic cloves, chopped

10 dried chillies, deseeded

3 lemon grass stalks, chopped

3 coriander roots

2.5 cm/1 inch piece of fresh root ginger, peeled and chopped

½ teaspoon coriander seeds, dry-fried

1 teaspoon cumin seeds, dry-fried

2 tablespoons Crushed Roasted Nuts (see page 24)

2 tablespoons groundnut oil

green curry paste

15 small fresh green chillies

4 garlic cloves, halved

2 lemon grass stalks, finely chopped

2 lime leaves, torn

2 shallots, chopped

50 g/2 oz fresh coriander leaves, stalks and roots

2.5 cm/1 inch piece of fresh root ginger, peeled and chopped

2 teaspoons coriander seeds

1 teaspoon black peppercorns

1 teaspoon peeled lime rind

½ teaspoon salt

2 tablespoons groundnut oil

- Put all the ingredients in a blender or food processor and blend to a thick paste.
- Alternatively, put the chillies in a mortar and crush with the pestle, then add the garlic and crush with the chillies, and so on with all the other ingredients, finally mixing in the oil with a spoon.
- Transfer the paste to an airtight container and store in the refrigerator for up to 3 weeks.

Preparation time: 15 minutes

Preparation time: 15 minutes

red curry paste

10 large fresh red chillies

2 teaspoons coriander seeds

5 cm/2 inch piece of galangal, peeled and finely chopped

1 lemon grass stalk, finely chopped

4 garlic cloves, halved

1 shallot, roughly chopped

1 teaspoon lime juice

2 tablespoons groundnut oil

○ Put all the ingredients in a blender or food processor and blend to a thick paste.

○ Alternatively, you can pound all the ingredients together with a mortar and pestle.

○ Transfer the paste to an airtight container and store in the refrigerator for up to 3 weeks.

rice
kao

There are several different methods of cooking rice. A great many Thais use electric rice steamers these days, but the following recipe has been used by people all over south-east Asia for centuries. I recommend using Thai jasmine or fragrant rice. Although it is more expensive than other long-grain rice, it is superb quality, tastes delicious and is what you would be eating were you in Thailand. I generally cook about 125 g/4 oz of rice per person, unless I am cooking several dishes, when I might cook only 50 g/2 oz or 75 g/3 oz per person.

500 g/1 lb Thai jasmine or
fragrant rice
1.8 litres/3 pints water

- Rinse the rice several times in a large bowl of water until the water is clear of rice starch. Drain thoroughly.
- Bring the measured water to the boil in a saucepan and put the rice into it, giving it a stir to ensure that the grains are not stuck together in clumps. Bring back to the boil and cook, stirring occasionally, for 5–6 minutes.
- Drain the rice into a metal colander and place it over another saucepan of boiling water, making sure that the level of the water is well beneath the rice. Take a chopstick and push it through the rice to the colander, to leave a steam hole. Do this in several places. Place a saucepan lid over the rice in the colander – it should not touch the rice – and steam for about 15 minutes, topping up the water level if necessary.
- Remove the lid, fluff up the rice a little with a fork and let it steam for 3–4 minutes more. It will now be ready to serve. You can cook your rice in this way, well in advance of your meal, and just leave it covered until 10 minutes before you need it, when you bring the water back to the boil and warm the rice again. You can also 'unfreeze' frozen rice quite quickly using this method.

Preparation time: 5 minutes
Cooking time: 20–25 minutes

Preparation time: 1–2 minutes
Cooking time: 3–5 minutes

ground roast rice

25 g/1 oz uncooked rice

- Dry-fry the rice in a frying pan, using no oil. Shake and stir it around constantly until it turns a lovely golden colour. Remove from the heat and allow to cool.
- Grind the rice using a mortar and pestle, or in a clean coffee or spice grinder.
- If you like, you can make a larger quantity, then store what you do not need immediately. Ground roast rice will keep up to 1 month in an airtight container in the refrigerator.

crispy basil

You can make Crispy Mint in the same way, using 25 g/1 oz fresh mint leaves.

2 tablespoons groundnut oil
25 g/1 oz fresh basil leaves
1 small fresh red chilli, finely
   sliced

- Heat the oil in a wok until it is hot, add the basil and chilli and stir-fry for 1 minute until crispy. Remove with a slotted spoon and drain on kitchen paper.

Preparation time: 2 minutes
Cooking time: 1 minute

Preparation time: 3 minutes

garlic oil

50 g/2 oz garlic, chopped
300 ml/½ pint groundnut oil
1 teaspoon ground black
  pepper

○ Put all the ingredients into an airtight container and leave to stand for 1 week before using.

crispy garlic and shallots

Thai people usually flavour their oil with garlic and shallots before using it. The crispy garlic and shallots are drained from the oil, reserved, and then sprinkled on to many different dishes. If you like, you can deep-fry just garlic or shallots, or you can deep-fry them both as here, then store them together rather than separately. It's all a matter of personal choice.

about 750 ml/1¼ pints
  groundnut oil, for deep-frying
25 g/1 oz garlic, finely chopped
25 g/1 oz shallots, finely
  chopped

○ Heat the oil for deep-frying in a wok. When the oil is good and hot, throw in the garlic and stir for about 40 seconds, watching it sizzle and turn golden.

○ Remove the garlic with a slotted spoon, draining as much oil as possible back into the wok, then spread the garlic out to dry on kitchen paper. Repeat the process with the shallots allowing 1½–2 minutes frying time.

○ When the garlic and shallots are dried and crispy, you can store them in separate airtight containers, where they will keep for up to 1 month.

○ When the groundnut oil is cold, return it to an airtight container, to be reused.

Preparation time: 5 minutes
Cooking time: 2–2½ minutes

Preparation time: 1–2 minutes
Cooking time: 3–5 minutes

crushed roasted nuts

25g/1oz unroasted peanuts or cashew nuts

- Dry-fry the nuts in a frying pan, using no oil. Stir them around constantly until they turn a lovely golden colour. Remove from the heat and allow to cool.
- Place the nuts in a plastic bag and break into small pieces using a rolling pin.
- You can roast and crush a larger quantity of nuts, then store what you do not need for up to 1 month in an airtight container in the refrigerator.

vegetable stock

2 large onions, quartered

4 large fresh red chillies

250 g/8 oz carrots, halved

¼ small white cabbage, halved

1 small head of celery (including leaves), chopped

50 g/2 oz fresh coriander leaves, stalks and roots

25 g/1 oz fresh basil leaves and stalks

½ head Chinese leaves, chopped

½ mooli radish, peeled

25 black peppercorns

½ teaspoon salt

1 teaspoon palm sugar or light muscovado sugar

2 litres/3½ pints water

- Put all the ingredients, including the water, into a large, heavy-bottomed saucepan or casserole. Bring to the boil, cover and simmer for 1 hour.
- Remove the lid and boil hard for 10 minutes. Allow to cool, then strain. Freeze any stock you are not using immediately.

Makes 1.8 litres/3 pints
Preparation time: 5–10 minutes
Cooking time: about 1 hour 30 minutes

Makes 2 litres/3½ pints
Preparation time: 3 minutes
Cooking time: 1 hour

fish stock

500 g/1 lb heads and bones of
  raw white fish and heads and
  shells of prawns, if available
2.4 litres/4 pints water
3 shallots
1 celery stalk, including leaves,
  roughly chopped
1 lime leaf
½ stalk lemon grass
2 garlic cloves
25 g/1 oz coriander stalks
  and roots

○ Put the fish heads and bones and water into a saucepan and bring to the boil. Skim off any scum that rises to the top.

○ Add the shallots, celery, lime leaf, lemon grass, garlic and coriander and simmer for 50 minutes.

○ Strain the stock and freeze what you do not need to use immediately.

chicken stock

1.75 kg/3½ lb boiling chicken
500 g/1 lb chicken giblets
1 onion, halved
1 carrot, roughly chopped
2 celery stalks, including leaves,
  roughly chopped
2 garlic cloves
1 stalk lemon grass, roughly
  chopped
10 black peppercorns
1.8 litres/3 pints water
1 lime leaf
3 large red chillies

○ Put the chicken into a large heavy-bottomed saucepan or casserole with the giblets, onion, carrot and celery and just cover them with the cold water. Place over a very low heat and bring to the boil as slowly as possible, about 50 minutes. When it begins to simmer, remove the scum from the top until only white foam rises.

○ Add the remaining ingredients and cook slowly for 2 hours, covered. Use a heat diffuser if you need to.

○ Remove the chicken and set aside for another use. Strain the stock without pressing the juices from the vegetables – this helps to keep it clear. You can use as much as you need immediately and freeze the rest for the future.

Makes 1.5 litres/2½ pints
Preparation time: 3 minutes
Cooking time: 2 hours 50 minutes

From left: crispy wrapped prawns; stuffed chicken wings (pages 28-29)

snacks
and *starters*

Thai people don't have the conception of starters that Westerners do – but they certainly eat lots of snacks. All day long the little food stalls that line the streets do a roaring trade – each one specializing in a few chosen dishes. One or other of these dishes might well appear as part of a Thai meal, but can equally well be served separately as a starter, if you prefer. Cook several of them for a light lunch or spear them with toothpicks and serve them as finger food at a party.

Preparation time: 10–15 minutes
Cooking time: 5 minutes

crispy wrapped prawns

kung hom pa

75 g/3 oz minced pork

4 raw prawns, shelled and minced

½ teaspoon sugar

¼ onion, finely chopped

1 garlic clove, finely chopped

2 teaspoons light soy sauce

12 raw prawns

12 spring roll wrappers

beaten egg white, for sticking

about 750 ml/1¼ pints oil, for deep-frying

sprig of basil or coriander, to garnish

Hot Sweet Sauce (see page 114), to serve

○ Mix the minced pork, 4 minced raw prawns, sugar, onion, garlic and soy sauce together in a bowl and set aside.

○ Shell the other 12 prawns, leaving the tails, and carefully cut them open, making sure you do not cut right through them, and keeping the shell-on tails intact.

○ Put 1 teaspoon or more of the minced mixture on to each opened prawn. Take a spring roll wrapper and pull one corner about ¾ of the way towards the opposite corner. Place a prawn on to the double thickness of wrapper, leaving the tail free, and roll it up, tucking the ends in and sticking it down with a little egg white. Continue until all prawns are wrapped.

○ Heat the oil in a wok and deep-fry the prawn rolls until golden – this should take about 5 minutes. Remove from the wok and drain on kitchen paper.

○ Garnish with basil or coriander and serve with hot sweet sauce.

Preparation time: 35 minutes
Cooking time: 21 minutes

stuffed chicken wings
peagai yat sai

8 chicken wings

175 g/6 oz minced pork

2 teaspoons palm sugar or
  light muscovado sugar

2½ tablespoons light soy sauce

pinch of black pepper

40 g/1½ oz onion, finely
  chopped

25 g/1 oz peas

50 g/2 oz rice vermicelli,
  soaked for 15–20 minutes
  and cut into 2.5 cm/1 inch
  lengths

about 750 ml/1¼ pints oil, for
  deep-frying

Hot Sweet Sauce (see page
  114), to serve

- Remove the main bones from the chicken wings by loosening the meat with a knife around the top, pulling it down over the bones and removing them.
- Place the minced pork, sugar, soy sauce, pepper, onion, peas and rice vermicelli in a bowl and mix them together thoroughly.
- Fill each wing with an equal amount of stuffing and pull the chicken meat shut at the end, enclosing the stuffing. The wings should now appear as they did before boning.
- Place the stuffed wings in a steamer and steam for 15 minutes.
- Heat the oil in a wok, transfer the wings from the steamer and deep-fry them until they are golden – about 6 minutes.
- Serve the wings with hot sweet sauce.

Preparation time: 10–15 minutes, plus marinating
Cooking time: 10 minutes

chicken satay
satay gai

500 g/1 lb chicken breast,
    thinly sliced into 2.5 cm/
    1 inch × 5 cm/2 inch slices
bamboo skewers, soaked in
    water for 30 minutes
Easy Satay Sauce (see page
    117), to serve

Marinade:
1 tablespoon ground
    cinnamon
1 tablespoon ground cumin
1 teaspoon ground black
    pepper
150 ml/¼ pint oil
100 ml/3½ fl oz light soy sauce
2 tablespoons palm sugar or
    light muscovado sugar

To garnish:
raw onion, roughly chopped
cucumber chunks

- Put the chicken slices into a container and add all the ingredients for the marinade. Stir very thoroughly and make sure that all the chicken pieces are coated in the marinade. Leave for a minimum of 4 hours, but preferably overnight. Give it an occasional stir.
- Carefully thread the chicken pieces on to the bamboo skewers, leaving some space at either end. Place them under a hot grill for about 2 minutes, turning once. As you cannot see if the chicken is cooked through, test one piece – you can always grill it for a little longer if necessary.
- You will have to cook the skewers in batches, so keep the cooked chicken warm whilst waiting for them all to be done.
- Garnish with chopped raw onion and chunks of cucumber and serve with easy satay sauce.

Preparation time: 12–14 minutes
Cooking time: 30 minutes

stuffed peppers
prik yat sai

4 peppers, red, green or yellow
5 garlic cloves
8 coriander roots
275 g/9 oz minced pork
1 tablespoon light soy sauce
½ teaspoon ground black
   pepper

To garnish:
Thai Egg Strips (see below)
coriander leaves

- Carefully core and deseed the peppers. Pound the garlic and coriander roots together in a mortar until well broken down, about 2–3 minutes.
- Place the pork in a bowl and add the garlic, coriander, soy sauce and pepper. Mix together thoroughly and leave to stand for 7–8 minutes.
- Fill the peppers with the pork mixture, then place in a steamer and steam for about 30 minutes.
- Remove the peppers to a dish and cut each one into 3–4 slices, arranging them so that they look whole.
- Serve garnished with egg strips and coriander leaves.

thai egg strips
kai tiaow

3 eggs, beaten
1 shallot, finely sliced
green shoots of 1 spring onion,
   sliced
1–2 small fresh red chillies,
   finely chopped
1 tablespoon chopped fresh
   coriander leaves
1 tablespoon groundnut oil
salt and pepper
julienne of spring onion,
   to garnish (optional)

- Mix all the ingredients, except the oil, in a bowl.
- Heat the oil in a frying pan or wok, pour in the egg mixture and swirl it around the pan to produce a large thin omelette. Cook for 1–2 minutes until firm.
- Slide the omelette out on to a plate and roll it up as though it were a pancake. Allow to cool.
- When the omelette is cool, cut the roll crossways into 5 mm/¼ inch or 1 cm/½ inch sections, depending on how wide you would like your strips to be. Serve them still rolled up or straightened out, in a heap. Garnish with strips of spring onion, if wished.

Preparation time: 5 minutes
Cooking time: 2–3 minutes

Preparation time: 20 minutes
Cooking time: 15 minutes

son-in-law eggs
kai luk kuhy

4 hard-boiled eggs

about 750 ml/1¼ pints groundnut oil, for deep-frying

5 shallots, finely sliced

3 large garlic cloves, finely
  sliced

75 ml/3 fl oz tamarind water

50 ml/2 fl oz fish sauce or
  1 teaspoon salt

60 g/2½ oz palm sugar or light
  muscovado sugar

100 ml/3½ fl oz water

To garnish:

2 large fresh red chillies,
  deseeded and sliced
  lengthways

fresh coriander leaves

- Shell the eggs and cut them in half lengthways.
- Heat the oil for deep-frying in a wok and add the shallots and garlic. Cook gently until golden. Remove with a slotted spoon, drain on kitchen paper and set aside.
- Slide the eggs, yolk side down, into the hot oil. Cook until golden all over, then remove with a slotted spoon. Drain and set aside.
- In a saucepan, put the tamarind water, fish sauce and sugar. Stir until the sugar has melted, then add the water. Cook for 5 minutes, stirring all the time until the sauce becomes syrupy. Lower the heat.
- Arrange the eggs, yolk side up, on a plate. Sprinkle the shallots and garlic over them. Bring the sauce to a hard boil and continue boiling until it is somewhat reduced and thickened. Remove the pan from the heat and then ladle the sauce over the eggs.
- Serve hot, garnished with the red chilli slivers and coriander leaves.

prawn and corn fritters
tod mun kung

20 g/¾ oz self-raising flour

65 g/2½ oz raw prawns,
  minced

1 teaspoon Red Curry Paste
  (see page 19)

50 g/2 oz corn kernels

1 egg white

1 lime leaf, shredded

oil, for deep-frying

coriander sprigs, to garnish
  (optional)

To serve:

Hot Sweet Sauce (see
  page 114)

Soy and Vinegar Dipping Sauce
  (see page 113)

- Mix the flour, minced prawns, red curry paste, corn kernels, egg white and lime leaf together thoroughly, in a bowl.
- Heat the oil in a wok over a moderate heat, then put 1 heaped tablespoon of the mixture at a time into the hot oil. You may want to do this in 2 batches. Cook until golden brown – about 5 minutes.
- Remove the fritters from the wok and drain on kitchen paper, then turn them on to a serving dish.
- Garnish with coriander, if using and serve with the dipping sauces.

Preparation time: 5 minutes
Cooking time: 10 minutes

prawn and pork toast
kanoom bung nar gung

about 750 ml/1¼ pints oil, for
  deep-frying

75 g/3 oz minced pork

8 raw prawns, minced

1 teaspoon sugar

¼ onion, finely chopped

2 large garlic cloves, finely
  chopped

1 tablespoon light soy sauce

1 egg

4 slices white bread

2 teaspoons sesame seeds

basil sprigs, to garnish

- Heat the oil in a wok and, while it is heating, mix the pork, prawns, sugar, onion, garlic, soy sauce and egg well together in a bowl. Spread the mixture on the bread and press sesame seeds on to it.
- Slide the bread into the wok, spread side up, 2 pieces at a time, and deep-fry on a moderate heat for about 5 minutes, or until golden. Turn each slice over and cook for 30 seconds, then remove from the oil and drain on kitchen paper.
- Cut each slice into 4 pieces, arrange on a serving dish and garnish with a few sprigs of basil.
- Serve with the dipping sauces.

Preparation time: 10 minutes
Cooking time: 11 minutes

To serve:

Hot Sweet Sauce (see
  page 114)

Soy and Vinegar Dipping Sauce
  (see page 113)

spring rolls *bapia tod*

12 square spring roll wrappers
about 750 ml/1¼ pints groundnut oil, for deep-frying
12 toothpicks
coriander leaves, to garnish
Lime and Fish Sauce and Hot
   Sweet Sauce (see page 114),
   to serve

Filling:

1 tablespoon groundnut oil
2 garlic cloves, finely chopped
50 g/2 oz bean sprouts
50 g/2 oz white cabbage,
   shredded
2 fresh shiitake mushrooms,
   shredded
20 g/¾ oz celery (leaf and
   stalk), finely chopped
1 teaspoon sugar
2 teaspoons soy sauce
50 g/2 oz dried bean thread
   noodles, soaked, drained and
   cut into short lengths with
   scissors

○ First make the filling: heat the wok and add the oil, garlic, bean sprouts, cabbage, mushrooms and celery. Stir-fry for 30 seconds, then add sugar, soy sauce and noodles. Stir-fry for 1 minute, then remove from the heat and place the ingredients on a plate. Wipe the wok clean with kitchen paper.

○ Put 1 tablespoon of the filling on one corner of a spring roll wrapper, then roll it up, wrapping in the ends to form a neat tube. Use a little oil to stick down the last corner, then secure the roll with a toothpick. Repeat with the remaining wrappers and filling.

○ Heat the oil for deep-frying in a wok, pop in a batch of spring rolls and cook over a moderate heat for 3–4 minutes until golden brown on all sides. Remove from the oil with a slotted spoon and drain on kitchen paper. Repeat with the remaining spring rolls.

○ Remove the toothpicks before serving and serve hot, with the dipping sauces in individual bowls and garnished with coriander leaves.

Preparation time: 15–20 minutes, plus soaking
Cooking time: 12 minutes

Preparation time: 15–20 minutes, plus soaking
Cooking time: 12 minutes

prawn spring rolls
bapia tod gung

12 square spring roll wrappers
about 750 ml/1¼ pints oil, for
    deep frying
12 toothpicks

Filling:
2 tablespoons oil
150 g/5 oz raw prawns, shelled
    and finely chopped
50 g/2 oz rice vermicelli,
    soaked for 15–20 minutes,
    drained and cut into short
    lengths
20 g/¾ oz grated carrot
40 g/1½ oz white cabbage,
    shredded
20 g/¾ oz bean sprouts
2 tablespoons light soy sauce
1 tablespoon sugar

To serve:
lettuce leaves
sliced tomatoes
Hot Sweet Sauce (see page
    114)

○ First make the filling: heat the oil in a wok, add the prawns, vermicelli, carrot, cabbage and bean sprouts and stir-fry for 1 minute. Add the soy sauce and sugar, stir-fry for 2 minutes, then remove from the heat and put the ingredients on a plate to cool. Wipe the wok clean with kitchen paper.

○ Put 1 tablespoon of the filling on to one corner of a spring roll wrapper and roll it up, tucking in the ends to form a neat tube. Use a little oil or egg white to stick down the last corner, then secure the roll with a toothpick.

○ Heat the oil for deep-frying in the wok and pop in the spring rolls, a few at a time. Cook them for 3–4 minutes until they are golden brown on all sides. Remove with a slotted spoon and drain on kitchen paper. Repeat with the remaining spring rolls.

○ Remove the toothpicks before serving. Place the spring rolls on a bed of lettuce leaves and sliced tomatoes and serve with the hot sweet sauce in a separate bowl.

Preparation time: 15 minutes
Cooking time: 30 minutes

steamed wonton
kanom jeeb

16 wonton wrappers
a little oil

Filling:
6 raw prawns, shelled
125 g/4 oz minced pork
40 g/1½ oz onion, chopped
2 garlic cloves
5 water chestnuts
1 teaspoon palm sugar or light
  muscovado sugar
1 tablespoon light soy sauce
1 egg

To serve:
Soy and Vinegar Dipping Sauce
  (see page 113)
Hot Sweet Sauce (see page
  114)

- To make the filling, blend all the ingredients in a blender or food processor.
- Put 1 heaped teaspoonful of the filling into the centre of a wrapper, placed over your thumb and index finger. As you push the filled wrapper down through the circle your fingers form, tighten the top, shaping it but leaving the top open. Repeat this process with all the wrappers.
- Put the filled wontons on to a plate and place the plate in a steamer. Drizzle a little oil on top of the wontons, put the lid on and steam for 30 minutes.
- Serve the wontons hot or warm, with the dipping sauces served separately.

soups

Soup is usually part of a Thai meal – even breakfast, which is often a rice soup. Noodle soups are eaten throughout south-East Asia as light meals in themselves. Cooked noodles are placed in the bowl first – they can be made of rice, bean or egg, and may be wide or narrow, dried or fresh – and then the bowl is filled with steaming stock. Next come pieces of chicken, pork or shrimps, meat or fish balls and the whole lot is garnished with coriander leaves, crispy shallots or garlic, sliced spring onions and chillies. Lighter soups form part of a whole meal. Thais don't drink with their meals as a rule and a few spoonfuls of soup now and then probably helps the rest of the meal go down!

Preparation time: 6 minutes
Cooking time: 10 minutes

chicken and coconut milk soup
tom ka gai

This quantity of soup is enough for 1 large bowl of soup shared between 4 people or 4 small, individual bowls. If you would like to serve the soup as a first course on its own, just double the quantities.

300 ml/½ pint Chicken Stock
  (see page 25)
3 lime leaves, torn
½ stalk lemon grass,
  obliquely sliced
2.5 cm/1 inch piece of galangal,
  peeled and finely sliced
100 ml/3½ fl oz coconut milk
4 tablespoons fish sauce
1 teaspoon palm sugar or light
  muscovado sugar
3 tablespoons lime juice
125 g/4 oz chicken, skinned
  and cut into bite-sized pieces
2 tablespoons chilli oil or
  2 small chillies, finely sliced
  (optional)

- Heat the stock and add the lime leaves, lemon grass and galangal. Stir them in and, as the stock is simmering, add the coconut milk, fish sauce, sugar and lime juice. Give it a good stir, then add the chicken pieces and simmer for 5 minutes.
- Just before serving, add the chilli oil or chillies, if you like, stir again and serve.

Preparation time: 5 minutes, plus soaking
Cooking time: 10 minutes

pork ball and black fungus soup

tom jieu won sen

This soup is usually served with Shrimp Paste Rice with Chicken (see page 105).

600 ml/1 pint Chicken Stock
  (see page 25)
2 garlic cloves, sliced
100 g/3½ oz minced pork
3 dried black fungi, soaked for
  30 minutes and sliced
2 tablespoons light soy sauce
1 tablespoon fish sauce
50 g/2 oz rice vermicelli,
  soaked for 15–20 minutes
  and cut into 5 cm/2 inch
  lengths

○ Heat the stock and add the garlic.
○ Shape the pork into little round balls. Drop them into the stock and simmer for 5 minutes.
○ Add the black fungus, soy sauce, fish sauce and rice vermicelli, cook for about 2 minutes and serve.

red pork noodle soup *ba mie mu daeng*

- Put the egg noodles into plenty of water and boil for 2–3 minutes, untangling them while they are boiling. Drain and mix in the garlic oil to prevent sticking.
- Boil the choi sum for 1 minute, drain and reserve.
- Place the noodles in a large serving bowl, then add the choi sum, spring onion, soy sauce, coriander leaves and black pepper. Arrange the pork slices on the top. Heat the chicken stock to boiling point and pour it over the pork, noodles and vegetables.
- Combine all the ingredients for the dipping sauce in a small bowl and serve with the soup.

Preparation time: 10 minutes
Cooking time: 5 minutes

175 g/6 oz fresh egg noodles
1 teaspoon Garlic Oil (see page 22)
2 choi sum, sliced
5 g/¼ oz spring onion, finely sliced
1 tablespoon light soy sauce
5 g/¼ oz coriander leaves
pinch of black pepper
200 g/7 oz Red Roast Pork, sliced (see page 58)
600 ml/1 pint Chicken Stock (see page 25)

Dipping sauce:
4 tablespoons distilled white vinegar
2–3 tablespoons fish sauce
1 large red chilli, sliced

pork and bamboo shoot soup *tom jieu moo sup nomai*

- Heat the stock then add the peppercorns and crushed and chopped garlic.
- Meanwhile, mix the pork with the pepper and soy sauce and form into small meat balls. Put them into the simmering stock and cook for 4 minutes. Add the bamboo shoots and simmer gently for 5 minutes. Add the fish sauce, give the soup a good stir, and serve, garnished with the spring onion and coriander leaves.

Preparation time: 6–8 minutes
Cooking time: 11 minutes

450 ml/¾ pint Chicken Stock (see page 25)
10 black peppercorns, crushed
2 garlic cloves, crushed
5 garlic cloves, roughly chopped
125 g/4 oz minced pork
pinch of black pepper
1½ tablespoons light soy sauce
100 g/3½ oz bamboo shoots
3 tablespoons fish sauce

To garnish:
1 spring onion, obliquely sliced
coriander leaves

Preparation time: 10 minutes
Cooking time: 12 minutes

noodle soup with chicken
kwetio nam gai

This soup is sufficient on its own for a light meal for 4 people. If you wish to serve it as part of a Thai meal, you should halve or even quarter the quantities.

- Put the stock, star anise, cinnamon, pickled garlic, vinegar, fish sauce, coriander, sugar and soy sauce into a large saucepan and bring slowly to the boil.
- Add the chicken and simmer for 4 minutes.
- Add the green vegetables and bean sprouts and simmer for 2 minutes.
- To serve, divide the rice sticks between 4 large soup bowls and ladle the soup over them. Sprinkle the coriander leaves on top and garnish with crispy shallots.

1.2 litres/2 pints Chicken Stock (see page 25)
1 star anise
7 cm/3 inch piece of cinnamon stick, broken up
2 bulbs Pickled Garlic (see page 110), finely chopped
4 tablespoons pickled garlic vinegar
125 ml/4 fl oz fish sauce
8 coriander roots, finely chopped
4 teaspoons palm sugar or light muscovado sugar
4 teaspoons light soy sauce
200 g/7 oz chicken, skinned and diced
125 g/4 oz green vegetables, such as spring cabbage, chard or pak choi, roughly chopped
50 g/2 oz bean sprouts
200 g/7 oz rice sticks, cooked
15 g/½ oz coriander leaves
Crispy Shallots (see page 22), to garnish

pork ball and tofu soup *tom jieu loo chin tahu*

600 ml/1 pint Chicken Stock (see page 25) or stock remaining from cooking Chicken with Rice (see page 71)

1 garlic clove, finely chopped

4 garlic cloves, halved

½ teaspoon ground black pepper

8 coriander roots

200 g/7 oz silken tofu, cut into 2.5 cm/1 inch slices

1 sheet roasted laver, torn into shreds

2 tablespoons light soy sauce

coriander leaves, to garnish

Pork balls:

65 g/2½ oz minced pork

1 tablespoon light soy sauce

½ teaspoon ground black pepper

- Heat the stock, with the chopped and halved garlic, pepper and coriander in a saucepan.
- While the soup is heating, make the pork balls. Mix together the pork, soy sauce and pepper, form the mixture into small balls, drop them into the soup and simmer gently for 6–7 minutes.
- Add the tofu, laver and soy sauce, stir for 30 seconds then serve, garnished with the coriander leaves.

Preparation time: 3–4 minutes
Cooking time: 12–13 minutes

Preparation time: 20 minutes, plus soaking
Cooking time: 20 minutes

mussel soup
tom jieu hoi

500 g/1 lb mussels

300 ml/½ pint coconut milk

600 ml/1 pint Fish Stock (see page 25)

75 g/3 oz rice vermicelli, soaked for 15–20 minutes

1 tablespoon finely chopped ginger

50 g/2 oz coriander stems and roots

½ stalk lemon grass, chopped

2 small red chillies, finely sliced

1 tablespoon fish sauce

1 tablespoon lime juice

25 g/1 oz coriander leaves, to garnish

- Clean the mussels thoroughly, remove the beards and leave to soak for about 1 hour in cold water. Drain and tap any open shells to ensure they close. If not, throw them away.
- Put the mussels into a saucepan, cover and cook over a moderate heat for 3–4 minutes. The mussels will open and release their liquid. Any that remain closed should be thrown away. Remove the mussels with a slotted spoon and reserve.
- Add the remaining ingredients and simmer for 15 minutes.
- Finally return the mussels to the pan and simmer for 1 minute. Serve, garnished with coriander leaves.

hot and sour prawn soup
tom yam kung

1.2 litres/2 pints Fish Stock (see page 25)

4 lime leaves, torn

1 stalk lemon grass, finely and obliquely sliced

2.5 cm/1 inch piece of galangal, sliced

1 tablespoon palm sugar or light muscovado sugar

5 tablespoons lime juice

2 tablespoons chilli oil or 12 small green chillies, chopped

12–16 raw prawns

salt and pepper

coriander sprigs, to garnish

- Place the stock, lime leaves, lemon grass, galangal, sugar, lime juice and chilli oil or chopped chillies in a large wok or saucepan and bring to the boil. Turn down the heat and allow the soup to simmer gently for 15 minutes.
- Add the prawns just before serving; they will turn pink in a few seconds and will be cooked through after 1 minute.
- Check the seasoning and serve the soup in one large bowl or individual bowls. Garnish with sprigs of coriander.

Preparation time: 5 minutes
Cooking time: 20 minutes

From left: beef curry country style; chilli pork (pages 52–53)

pork
and *beef*

Meat is really still food for a special occasion throughout most of Thailand. Beef is much less common than pork; there are few cattle in the country and a lot of the indigenous 'beef' is actually buffalo. The diet is all the healthier for the small quantities of meat, although every now and again for a feast day or a celebration of some kind, a lot of meat is served and you probably wouldn't be able to recognize most of it! Pork appears in numerous forms and in very different styles. For example, there is a spicy pork sausage that is common to northern Thailand, which is not found in many other parts of the country except, of course, Bangkok, to which people from all over Thailand migrate in search of a better life, bringing their local delicacies with them.

Preparation time: 10 minutes
Cooking time: 6–8 minutes

chilli pork
nam prik ong

5 small shallots

15 g/½ oz large dried chillies,
   soaked for 20 minutes

12 coriander roots

3 tablespoons oil

125 g/4 oz minced pork

2 tomatoes, diced

5 teaspoons sugar

5 teaspoons fish sauce

coriander leaves, to garnish

Salad:

½ cucumber, cut into chunks

1 little gem lettuce, separated
   into leaves

coriander sprigs

○ Put the shallots, chillies and coriander roots into a food processor or blender and blend, adding a little water if the mixture seems very dry. Alternatively, pound them together in a mortar for 5–8 minutes until thoroughly amalgamated.

○ Heat the oil in a wok, add the chilli paste and stir-fry for 30 seconds. Add the pork and tomatoes and cook, stirring, for 30 seconds, then add the sugar and fish sauce and continue to cook, stirring, for 4–5 minutes.

○ Turn the pork into a bowl, garnish with coriander and serve, with the salad arranged on a separate plate.

Preparation time: 8 minutes
Cooking time: 17 minutes

beef curry country style
gang bar nua

1 tablespoon oil

2 tablespoons Red Curry
Paste (see page 19)

125 g/4 oz lean rump steak,
cut into thin, bite-sized pieces

30 g/1¼ oz krachai, washed
and cut into fine julienne
strips

300 ml/½ pint Chicken Stock
(see page 25)

3 tablespoons fish sauce

3 tablespoons palm sugar or
light muscovado sugar

125 g/4 oz baby corn,
obliquely sliced

75 g/3 oz sugar snap peas

125 g/4 oz bamboo shoots

1 or 2 large red chillies,
obliquely sliced

15 g/½ oz basil, chopped

○ Heat the oil in a wok and add the curry paste, beef and krachai and cook, stirring well, for 30 seconds. Add the stock and cook over a moderate heat for 2–3 minutes, stirring all the time, then add the fish sauce and sugar. Reduce the heat to low and cook for 10 more minutes.

○ Turn the heat to high and add all the vegetables and the chilli, stirring and turning for about 3 minutes. Add a little more stock if necessary.

○ To serve, add the basil, stir it in and turn the curry into a serving bowl.

Preparation time: 20 minutes
Cooking time: 9 minutes

pork with salted eggs and bean sprouts

pad tua nok kai kem moo

2 tablespoons oil

1 garlic clove, chopped

75 g/3 oz minced pork

1 tablespoon oyster sauce

1 teaspoon sugar

4 tablespoons Chicken Stock
  (see page 25)

1 tablespoon fish sauce

2 Salted Eggs – chicken or
  duck (see page 112), shelled
  and halved

200 g/7 oz bean sprouts

2 large red chillies, obliquely
  sliced

1 spring onion, obliquely sliced

coriander leaves, to garnish

- Allow the hard-boiled salted eggs to cool. Heat the oil in a wok and cook the garlic and pork for 3 minutes. Add the oyster sauce, sugar, stock and fish sauce and stir-fry for 5 minutes.
- Add the salted eggs and the remaining ingredients and cook very briefly – about 1 minute – then transfer to a serving dish.
- Serve, garnished with coriander leaves.

pork with lime
moo manao

300 g/10 oz loin of pork, cut
into 2.5 cm/1 inch × 1 cm/
½ inch strips
2 tablespoons light soy sauce
½ teaspoon ground black
pepper
1 tablespoon oil
10 garlic cloves, chopped
15 small green chillies,
chopped
4 tablespoons lime juice
4 tablespoons fish sauce
1 tablespoon palm sugar or
light muscovado sugar
15 g/½ oz mint leaves, finely
chopped

In Thailand, the garlic in this dish is not cooked. However you can fry it with the pork, if you prefer.

- Mix the pork, soy sauce and pepper together in a bowl.
- Heat the oil in a wok and add the pork mixture. Stir-fry, continuously turning and stirring, over a high heat, until the pork is well cooked – about 6 minutes.
- Transfer the pork to a mixing bowl or saucepan and add all the rest of the ingredients. Mix thoroughly, 1–2 minutes, then turn into a serving dish.

Preparation time: 10–12 minutes
Cooking time: 6 minutes

steamed egg with minced pork
kai toon moo sup

100 g/3½ oz minced pork
3 eggs
150 ml/¼ pint water
1 tablespoon oil
1½ tablespoons fish sauce
15 g/½ oz coriander leaves,
chopped
15 g/½ oz spring onion,
obliquely sliced
black pepper
Crispy Garlic and Shallots (see
page 22), to garnish

- Put the pork into a mixing bowl and break it up with a fork. Beat the eggs together and combine well with the pork; add the water, oil and fish sauce, season with pepper and mix it all together thoroughly.
- Transfer the pork mixture to a heat-proof bowl, sprinkle the coriander and spring onion on top, and steam, covered, for 40 minutes.
- To serve, sprinkle crispy garlic and shallots over the coriander and spring onion.

Preparation time: 5 minutes
Cooking time: 40 minutes

Preparation time: 10 minutes
Cooking time: 7 minutes

pork-stuffed omelette
kai yat sai moo

1 tablespoon oil
5 eggs, beaten
coriander sprigs, to garnish

Filling:

25 g/1 oz onion, finely
  chopped
1 small red chilli, finely sliced
1 cm/½ inch lemon grass,
  finely sliced
2 tablespoons oil
50 g/2 oz minced pork
1½ tomatoes, diced
25 g/1 oz mixed green, red
  and yellow peppers, finely
  chopped
15 g/½ oz sweetcorn kernels
15 g/½ oz peas
5 tablespoons Easy Sweet and
  Sour Sauce (see page 116)

○ First make the filling. Pound the onion, chilli and lemon grass in a mortar until well broken down then set aside.

○ Heat the oil in a wok, add the onion mixture, stir-fry for 30 seconds then add all the remaining ingredients and stir-fry for 2 minutes over a high heat.

○ Remove the filling from the wok and set aside.

○ Wipe the wok clean with kitchen paper.

○ To make the omelette, put the 1 tablespoon of oil into the wok and heat it, making sure the oil coats not only the base of the wok but as much of the sides as possible. Pour in the beaten eggs, swirling them around to make a large thin omelette.

○ When the omelette is almost firm, add the filling and fold the edges over to form a square parcel. Make sure the parcel does not stick to the bottom of the pan.

○ Carefully slide the omelette on to a serving plate, garnish with coriander and serve at once.

Preparation time: 5 minutes, plus marinating
Cooking time: 1–1¼ hours
Oven temperature: 200°C (400°F), Gas Mark 6

red roast pork
mu daeng

750 g/1½ lb pork shoulder,
  spare rib joint or leg, boned
  and rolled, with fat removed
1 packet (50 g/2 oz) red roast
  pork seasoning mix
1 tablespoon tomato purée
2 tablespoons palm sugar or
  light muscovado sugar
1 tablespoon Chicken Stock
  (see page 25)

To garnish:
coriander leaves
fresh chillies

I think it is worth making a large quantity of this as it can be used in many other dishes (see page 44) and is delicious cold as well as hot. However if you prefer, you can simply halve the quantities in the recipe and you will have sufficient for 4 people as part of a Thai meal.

- Cut the pork into 4 large chunks, put them into a bowl and mix in all the other ingredients thoroughly, making sure that all the pork is coated. Cover and leave to marinate for a minimum of 5 hours, preferably overnight.
- Place the pork in a roasting tin and cook in a preheated oven, 200°C (400°F), Gas Mark 6, for 1–1¼ hours, turning occasionally.
- To serve, slice the pork thinly, arrange on a serving dish and garnish with coriander leaves.

pork with bamboo shoots
moo nomai

2 tablespoons oil
1 tablespoon Red Curry Paste
  (see page 19)
150 ml/¼ pint Chicken Stock
  (see page 25)
125 g/4 oz pork, cut into bite-
  sized pieces
1 tablespoon palm sugar or
  light muscovado sugar
2 tablespoons fish sauce
100 g/3½ oz bamboo shoots
2 lime leaves, torn

- Heat the oil in a wok, add the red curry paste and cook for 30 seconds.
- Add the stock, pork, sugar and fish sauce and cook, stirring, for 4–5 minutes. Increase the heat, add the bamboo shoots and continue to cook for 1–2 minutes then add the lime leaves.
- Give the pork a final stir, turn into a bowl and serve at once.

Preparation time: 4 minutes
Cooking time: 9–10 minutes

Preparation time: 2–3 minutes, plus marinating
Cooking time: 40 minutes
Oven temperature: 180°C (350°F), Gas Mark 4

spare ribs
gat doog moo

4 large or 8 small pork spare ribs, weighing about 475 g/15 oz in total

Marinade:

1½ tablespoons palm sugar or light muscovado sugar

3 tablespoons light soy sauce

1 tablespoon oyster sauce

1 teaspoon ground black pepper

6 large garlic cloves, peeled and chopped

- Mix together all the marinade ingredients in a bowl. Add the spare ribs, turning them thoroughly to coat them all over with the marinade. The longer you leave them the tastier they will be, but they will need a minimum of 2 hours.
- Place the spare ribs on a baking sheet, with as much of the marinade as possible, and cook in a preheated oven, 180°C (350°F), Gas Mark 4, for 40 minutes.

sweet and sour
pork *peao wun moo*

2 tablespoons oil

125 g/4 oz pork, cut into thin slices

¾ onion, sliced

1 tomato, quartered

¼ cucumber, cut into chunks

50 g/2 oz fresh pineapple, cut into chunks

25 g/1 oz green or red pepper, thinly sliced

100 ml/3½ fl oz Easy Sweet and Sour Sauce (see page 116)

- Heat the oil in a wok. Add the pork and onion and stir-fry over a high heat for about 2 minutes.
- Add the tomato, cucumber, pineapple and green or red pepper and stir-fry for another 3 minutes.
- Add the sweet and sour sauce, mix well, stirring constantly for 1 minute, and serve at once.

Preparation time: 10 minutes
Cooking time: 6 minutes

Preparation time: 5 minutes
Cooking time: 14 minutes

panang beef curry
gang panang nua

1 tablespoon oil

1½ tablespoons Panang Curry Paste (see page 18)

6 tablespoons coconut milk

3 lime leaves, finely shredded

125 g/4 oz beef topside, cut into bite-sized pieces

3 tablespoons Chicken Stock (see page 25)

1 large red chilli, obliquely sliced

3 tablespoons palm sugar or light muscovado sugar

50 g/2 oz peas

2 lime leaves, torn, to garnish

- Heat the oil in a wok, add the curry paste and cook for 30 seconds.
- Pour in the coconut milk and add the lime leaves and stir and cook for 1 minute.
- Add the beef, stock, chilli and sugar and increase the heat and cook, stirring, for 1 minute, then reduce the heat and simmer for 7 minutes.
- Add the peas and simmer for 3 more minutes. The sauce should thicken considerably but add a little more stock if you feel it is getting too dry.
- Turn the curry into a serving bowl and serve garnished with lime leaves.

stir-fried beef with oyster sauce
nua pad nam mon hoi

2 tablespoons oil

125 g/4 oz rump steak, thinly sliced and cut into bite-sized pieces

1 garlic clove, peeled and chopped

40 g/1½ oz onion, sliced

25 g/1 oz mixed green, red and yellow peppers, thinly sliced

50 g/2 oz fresh shiitake mushrooms

1½ tablespoons oyster sauce

4 tablespoons Chicken Stock (see page 25)

1 large red chilli, obliquely sliced

1 teaspoon palm sugar or light muscovado sugar

15 g/½ oz spring onion, obliquely sliced

pinch of black pepper

- Heat the oil in a wok, add the beef, garlic, onion, mixed peppers and mushrooms and stir-fry over a fairly high heat for 2 minutes.
- Add the oyster sauce, stock, chilli and sugar and stir-fry for 2 minutes then add the spring onion and season with pepper.
- To serve, turn on to a serving platter.

Preparation time: 8–10 minutes
Cooking time: 5 minutes

Preparation time: 2 minutes
Cooking time: 6 minutes (for medium rare)

grilled beef with spicy sauce

neua yang nam tok

300 g/10 oz sirloin steak

Spicy sauce:

½ tomato, finely chopped

¼ red onion, finely chopped

1 tablespoon dried ground
  chilli

6 tablespoons fish sauce

2 tablespoons lime juice or
  tamarind water

2 teaspoons palm sugar or
  light muscovado sugar

1 teaspoon Ground Roast Rice
  (see page 21)

1 tablespoon Chicken Stock
  (see page 25)

To garnish:

basil leaves

coriander leaves

flat leaf parsley

chillies

- Put the steak under a preheated hot grill and cook, turning it once, according to your taste.
- While it is cooking, mix together all the sauce ingredients in a bowl.
- When the steak is ready, slice it up and arrange on a serving dish and garnish with the basil, coriander leaves, parsley and chillies. Serve the sauce separately.

Chickens and ducks in Thailand do not have much in common with those we usually eat here – they are smaller, thinner and tougher. However, unlike our tender but usually rather bland-tasting birds, these taste superb. They spend their lives roaming around freely, feeding on whatever they find. Ducks splash about the paddy fields happily. Chicken and duck are often chopped up before cooking. I suggest asking your butcher to do this for you – unless you are quite skilled you will find the bones splinter when you do it yourself. Thais do not generally skin their chicken but I think that is a matter of personal preference. It is worth removing as much fat as you can though, as all the recipes contain some oil or coconut milk as well.

chicken
and *duck*

Preparation time: 5–7 minutes
Cooking time: 13–15 minutes

green curry chicken
gang keyo wun gai

1 tablespoon oil
1½ tablespoons Green Curry
  Paste (see page 18)
4 tablespoons coconut milk
125 g/4 oz chicken breast, cut
  into bite-sized pieces
2 lime leaves, torn
½ stalk lemon grass, cut in fine,
  oblique slices
50 g/2 oz bamboo shoots
3 small round green
  aubergines, cut into quarters
50 g/2 oz courgette, cut in
  oblique chunks
1 large red chilli, obliquely
  sliced
6 tablespoons Chicken Stock
  (see page 25)
1 tablespoon palm sugar or
  light muscovado sugar
3 tablespoons fish sauce
sweet basil sprigs, to garnish

○ Heat the oil in a wok and stir in the curry paste. Cook for 30 seconds, then add the coconut milk and cook, stirring, for 1 minute.

○ Add the chicken, bring up to a simmer and add all the remaining ingredients. Simmer for 10 minutes, stirring occasionally.

○ Transfer the curry to a serving bowl, garnish with basil sprigs and serve.

Preparation time: 15 minutes
Cooking time: 6 minutes

chilli fried duck
pad pet prik

¼ roast duck

2 tablespoons oil

3 large garlic cloves, peeled
   and finely chopped

½ onion, sliced

25 g/1 oz carrot, sliced

50 g/2 oz mixed green, red
   and yellow peppers, sliced

3 baby corn cobs, obliquely
   sliced

1 broccoli floret, chopped

4 sugar snap peas or
   mangetout

2 small green chillies, finely
   sliced

1 teaspoon palm sugar or light
   muscovado sugar

2 tablespoons light soy sauce

3 tablespoons Chicken Stock
   (see page 25)

basil leaves, to garnish

- Take the skin and meat off the duck, chop into bite-sized pieces and set aside.
- Heat the oil in a wok, add the garlic and stir-fry for 10 seconds. Add the duck, stir briefly and then add the onion, carrot, mixed peppers, corn cobs, broccoli and sugar snap peas or mangetout. Stir-fry vigorously for 20 seconds, add the chilli and cook, stirring, for 45 seconds.
- Finally, add the sugar, light soy sauce and chicken stock, mixing them thoroughly with the contents of the wok for 3 minutes.
- Turn on to a serving dish and garnish with basil leaves.

Preparation time: 6 minutes
Cooking time: 6 minutes

minced chicken with basil

pad grapao gai

5 small green chillies
2 garlic cloves
2 tablespoons oil
125 g/4 oz minced chicken
1 shallot, chopped
25 g/1 oz bamboo shoots
25 g/1 oz red pepper, chopped
15 g/½ oz carrot, diced
1 teaspoon palm sugar or light
  muscovado sugar
3 tablespoons fish sauce
3 tablespoons Chicken Stock
  (see page 25)
15 g/½ oz basil leaves, finely
  chopped

To garnish:
Crispy Garlic (see page 22)
Crispy Shallots (see page 22)
Crispy Basil (see page 21)

- Put the chillies and garlic into a mortar and pound together with a pestle until well broken down.
- Heat the oil in a wok, add the chillies and garlic and stir-fry for 30 seconds. Add the remaining ingredients and cook, stirring, for 4 minutes over a medium heat. Turn the heat up high and continue stirring vigorously for 30 seconds.
- Turn on to a dish and serve with rice, garnished with crispy garlic, crispy shallots and crispy basil.

Preparation time: 10 minutes
Cooking time: 12–14 minutes

stir-fried chicken with pineapple
gai pad sapparote

about 750 ml/1¼ pints oil, for
    deep-frying
50 g/2 oz tempura flour or
    self-raising flour
75 ml/3 fl oz water
125 g/4 oz chicken, skinned
    and cut into bite-sized pieces
1 tablespoon oil
150 g/5 oz fresh pineapple, cut
    into chunks
1 tomato, cut into 8 pieces
1 tablespoon tomato purée
1 tablespoon palm sugar or
    light muscovado sugar
50 g/2 oz cashew nuts
1½ tablespoons light soy sauce

To garnish:
1 spring onion, obliquely sliced
coriander sprigs

- Heat the oil in a wok and, while it is heating, mix the flour and water together thoroughly to make a coating batter.
- When the oil is hot enough, coat half the chicken pieces in the batter and deep-fry them until they are golden brown. Remove from the oil and drain them on kitchen paper. Repeat the process with the rest of the chicken.
- Pour off the oil, wipe the wok clean with kitchen paper then heat 1 tablespoon of oil in it. Add the pineapple, tomato, tomato purée, sugar and cashews, and stir-fry for 2 minutes.
- Add the soy sauce and stir, put back the batter-coated chicken and stir again over a high heat then serve, garnished with spring onion and coriander sprigs.

stir-fried chicken with ginger
gai pad king

- Heat the oil in a wok, add the onion, garlic and chicken and stir-fry for about 2 minutes. Add the ginger and mushrooms and continue to stir-fry over a gentle heat for 2½ minutes. Add the oyster sauce, yellow beans, sugar and stock, turn up the heat and stir-fry for 30 seconds.
- Turn on to a serving dish, sprinkle with spring onion and serve.

Preparation time: 5 minutes
Cooking time: 5 minutes

2 tablespoons oil
¼ onion, chopped
2 garlic cloves, peeled and chopped
125 g/4 oz boneless, skinless chicken, in bite-sized pieces
25 g/1 oz julienne ginger
3 fresh shiitake mushrooms, sliced
1 tablespoon oyster sauce
1 tablespoon yellow beans
1 teaspoon palm sugar or light muscovado sugar
3 tablespoons Chicken Stock (see page 25)
1 spring onion, obliquely sliced, to garnish

chicken with rice
kao man gai

- Skin the chicken and remove as much fat as you can. Place the chicken and skin in a casserole with enough water to cover then add the coriander and garlic and boil, covered, until cooked, about 1 hour. Reduce the heat to a minimum.
- Put the rice into a heavy-bottomed saucepan and ladle over enough stock from the chicken pan to cover it. The liquid should be 5 mm/¼ inch above the level of the rice. Bring the rice to the boil over a moderate heat, stir to make sure it does not stick together in lumps and simmer, uncovered, until the rice has absorbed all the stock. Then, lower the heat as much as you can, cover tightly and leave for 10–12 minutes.
- Take the rice off the heat and leave it, still covered, for another 3–4 minutes.
- Meanwhile, make the sauce. Put the garlic, ginger, yellow beans in salted sauce, chillies and coriander into a food processor and blend. Pour the mixture into a bowl and mix in the stock, lime juice, light soy sauce and sugar. Now pile the rice on to the plates, carve the chicken and arrange it on top of the rice and serve, garnished with coriander leaves, and with the sauce separately.
- This dish is traditionally served with Pork Ball and Tofu Soup (see page 47).

Preparation time: 20 minutes
Cooking time: 1 hour 20 minutes

1.5 kg/3 lb chicken
1 sprig coriander, including stalk and root
1 large garlic clove, chopped
575 g/1 lb 3 oz rice, washed
coriander leaves, to garnish

Sauce:
40 g/1½ oz garlic cloves
40 g/1½ oz julienne ginger
1 heaped tablespoon yellow beans in salted sauce
4 large red chillies, halved
15 g/½ oz coriander stalk and root
2 tablespoons Chicken Stock (see page 25)
3 tablespoons lime juice
3 tablespoons light soy sauce
1 tablespoon sugar

Preparation time: 6 minutes
Cooking time: 5–6 minutes

stir-fried chicken with cashew nuts and baby corn

gai pad met mamuang hin ma parn

3 tablespoons oil

125 g/4 oz chicken, skinned and cut into bite-sized pieces

¼ onion, sliced

50 g/2 oz baby corn, obliquely sliced

50 g/2 oz cashew nuts

125 ml/4 fl oz light soy sauce

4 tablespoons Chicken Stock (see page 25)

4 teaspoons palm sugar or light muscovado sugar

15 g/½ oz spring onion, obliquely sliced

ground black pepper

1 large red chilli, obliquely sliced, to garnish

- Heat the oil in a wok, add the chicken, onion, baby corn and cashew nuts. Stir-fry over a high heat for 3 minutes.
- Reduce the heat and stir in the soy sauce. Then add the stock, sugar, spring onion and season with black pepper. Raise the heat and stir-fry for another 2 minutes.
- Turn on to a serving dish, sprinkle with sliced chilli and serve.

Preparation time: 6 minutes, plus marinating
Cooking time: 15 minutes

coconut grilled chicken
gai yarn maprow

This dish will serve four as part of a Thai meal but if you plan to serve it in western style, with rice and a salad, allow one chicken breast for each person.

2–3 chicken breasts, boned

Marinade:

400 ml/14 fl oz can coconut milk

4 garlic cloves

4 small green or red chillies

2.5 cm/1 inch piece of fresh root ginger, peeled and sliced

grated rind and juice of 1 lime

2 tablespoons palm sugar or light muscovado sugar

3 tablespoons light soy sauce

1 tablespoon fish sauce

25 g/1 oz coriander leaf, stalk and root

To garnish:

red chilli, finely diced

spring onion slivers

- To make the marinade, blend together all the ingredients.
- Make 3 oblique cuts on each side of the chicken breasts, place them in a dish and pour over the marinade. Cover and leave them in the refrigerator for 2 hours.
- Preheat the grill and arrange the chicken pieces in the grill pan, making sure they are fairly thickly spread with the marinade. Grill for about 15 minutes, turning occasionally. The skin side will take a little longer than the other side.
- Meanwhile, heat the remaining marinade, adding a little of the chicken stock if it is too thick.
- When the chicken is cooked, cut it into slices and arrange on a serving dish.
- Serve the chicken garnished with spring onion slivers and diced chilli, with the sauce in a separate bowl.

Preparation time: 12–15 minutes
Cooking time: 5 minutes

red curry duck
gaeng pet ped yaung

¼ roast duck

1 tablespoon oil

1½ tablespoons Red Curry
Paste (see page 19)

150 ml/¼ pint coconut milk

1 tablespoon palm sugar or
light muscovado sugar

3 lime leaves, torn

65 g/2½ oz peas – fresh or
frozen

1 large red chilli, obliquely
sliced

4 tablespoons Chicken Stock
(see page 25)

1½ tomatoes, quartered

125 g/4 oz fresh or tinned
pineapple, cut into chunks

1 tablespoon fish sauce

○ Take the skin and meat off the duck, chop it into bite-sized pieces and set aside.

○ Heat the oil in a wok, add the red curry paste and fry, stirring, for 30 seconds. Add 3 tablespoons of the coconut milk, amalgamate it with the paste, then add the remainder and stir over a gentle heat for 1 minute.

○ Add the duck and stir for 2 minutes. Add the sugar, lime leaves, peas, chilli, chicken stock, tomatoes and pineapple. Mix well together and finally, with the curry simmering, add the fish sauce. Give it all a good stir, transfer the contents of the wok into a bowl and serve.

Preparation time: 20 minutes
Cooking time: 10 minutes

duck paolo
pet paolo

¼ roast duck
1 tablespoon oil
1 tablespoon chopped garlic
½ teaspoon ground black
  pepper
2 tablespoons paolo powder
600 ml/1 pint Chicken Stock
  (see page 25)
2 x 2.5 cm/1 inch pieces
  cinnamon stick
2 star anise
2 eggs, hard-boiled and shelled
20 g/¾ oz coriander leaf, stalk
  and root
1 teaspoon dark soy sauce
1 tablespoon palm sugar or
  light muscovado sugar
3 tablespoons light soy sauce

○ Take the skin and meat off the duck, chop it into bite-sized pieces and set aside.

○ Heat the oil in a wok, add the garlic and black pepper and stir-fry until the garlic begins to turn golden. Add the paolo powder, stir well and pour in the chicken stock. Add the cinnamon and star anise and bring gently to the boil, stirring. Add the duck and eggs and turn the heat down to a simmer.

○ Take the stalk and root from the coriander and cut into small pieces, reserving the leaves, and add them, with the dark soy sauce, sugar and light soy sauce. Stir well and allow to simmer for 3 minutes.

○ Remove the eggs with a slotted spoon and halve them.

○ Transfer the contents of the wok to a serving bowl, taking care to arrange the eggs, yolk side up, around the edge. Garnish with the reserved coriander leaves.

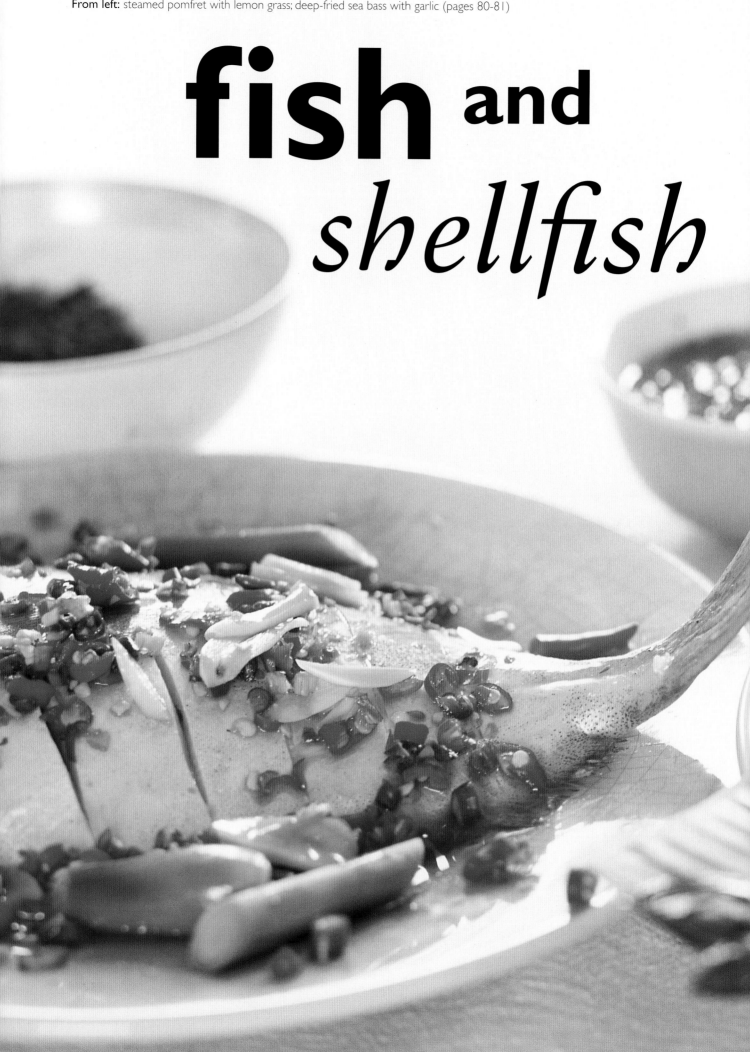

From left: steamed pomfret with lemon grass; deep-fried sea bass with garlic (pages 80-81)

fish and *shellfish*

Thailand abounds with fish and shellfish. The protein derived from them is essential, and even the very poorest people can eat rice mixed with shrimp paste and soups flavoured with fish sauce. The sea is still full of fish, though not as many as there were, as are the rivers, and fish and shellfish farms are ever increasing. Southern Thailand is the region most famed for its seafood and for its use of coconut milk and flesh – coconut palms grow widely throughout the region.

Preparation time: 15–20 minutes
Cooking time: 40 minutes

deep-fried sea bass with garlic

pla kapong tod kratiem

about 750 ml/1¼ pints oil, for
  deep frying
1 × 625 g/1¼ lb whole sea
  bass, cleaned
15 garlic cloves, sliced
2 tablespoons oil
2 tablespoons palm sugar or
  light muscovado sugar
1 tablespoon light soy sauce

Sauce:
7 small green chillies
3 garlic cloves
5 tablespoons fish sauce
3 tablespoons lime juice
1 teaspoon palm sugar or light
  muscovado sugar
15 g/½ oz coriander leaf, stalk
  and root, chopped

To garnish:
spring onion slivers
red chillies

○ Heat the oil in a wok and fry the fish for about 25 minutes. Turn it over carefully and cook for a further 10 minutes, or until really crispy. Remove the fish from the oil and drain on kitchen paper.

○ Set the wok aside for the oil to cool then pour off the oil and reserve to use another time.

○ While the fish is cooking make the sauce. Put the chillies into a mortar and pound for 1 minute, then add the garlic and pound together for 2 minutes or until well broken down and combined with the chillies. Add the remaining sauce ingredients, one by one, pounding after each addition, then pour the sauce into a bowl and set aside.

○ Slice the 15 garlic cloves. Wipe the wok clean with kitchen paper.

○ Put the 2 tablespoons of oil into the wok, add the garlic and stir-fry for 3–5 minutes until golden and crispy. Turn off the heat and add the sugar and soy sauce, giving it a good stir.

○ Place the fish on a serving dish and top with the garlic. Garnish with the spring onion and chilli and serve with the sauce.

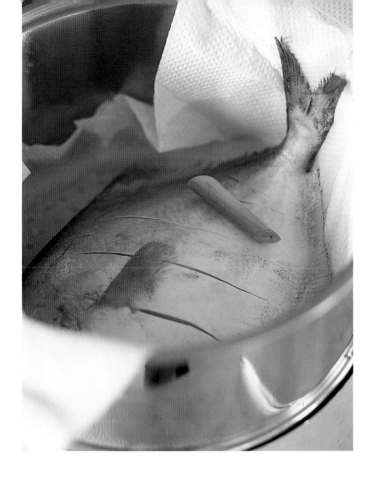

steamed pomfret with lemon grass
pla neung ma now

1 × 375 g/12 oz pomfret, cleaned

1 teaspoon salt

1 stalk lemon grass, cut into 3 pieces

15 small red and green chillies

1 coriander root, crushed and chopped

3 garlic cloves, finely sliced

3 tablespoons fish sauce

2 tablespoons light soy sauce

ground dried chilli, to serve

- Cut oblique slashes on each side of the fish and rub the salt all over it to firm it up. Leave for 2 minutes then wash off the salt.
- Place the fish on a plate, arrange the lemon grass on top then put it into a steamer, and steam for 35–40 minutes.
- Meanwhile, chop the chillies very finely and put them into a small bowl with the crushed and chopped coriander, garlic, fish and soy sauces and stir thoroughly.
- To serve, pour the sauce over the fish and serve with the ground chilli on the side.

Preparation time: 5 minutes
Cooking time: 35–40 minutes

Preparation time: 3 minutes
Cooking time: 12 minutes

crab curry
gang pet poo

1 tablespoon oil
1½ teaspoons Red Curry Paste
  (see page 19)
6 tablespoons coconut milk
1 lime leaf, torn
12 crab claws
150 ml/¼ pint Fish Stock (see
  page 25)
2 tablespoons sugar
1 teaspoon salt
65 g/2½ oz bamboo shoots

To garnish:
½ large red chilli, obliquely
  sliced
coriander leaves

- Heat the oil in a wok, add the curry paste and stir-fry for 30 seconds then add all the remaining ingredients. Stir well and simmer for 10 minutes. If the liquid level reduces significantly, add more stock.
- Turn into a bowl and serve, garnished with the chilli and coriander leaves.

steamed seafood curry *hor mok talay*

8 raw prawns, shelled but tails
  left intact
4 crab claws
75 g/3 oz crab meat
2 lime leaves, finely shredded
2.5 cm/1 inch lemon grass,
  finely sliced
1 egg, beaten
1 tablespoon Red Curry Paste
  (see page 19)
100 ml/3½ fl oz coconut milk
75 g/3 oz chopped Chinese
  leaves
25 g/1 oz chopped cabbage
1 teaspoon palm sugar or light
  muscovado sugar
2 tablespoons fish sauce
1 large red chilli, obliquely
  sliced
30 g/1¼ oz basil leaves
1 lime leaf, shredded

In Thailand this dish is usually steamed inside a young coconut. If you can buy one from your local oriental shop, you cut out a lid and a piece from the bottom to give the coconut a flat base. Follow the recipe but put the curry into the coconut, replace the lid and steam for 30 minutes. Then sprinkle the lime leaf on to the curry, replace the lid and steam for a further 30 minutes. Check that the curry is fully cooked – leave it to steam longer if not – and serve it from the coconut as the centrepiece of your dinner party.

- Mix all the ingredients together thoroughly in a heatproof bowl, except for the 1 shredded lime leaf, and steam, covered, for 10 minutes.
- Remove the lid, sprinkle the lime leaf on the curry, then replace the lid and steam for a further 25 minutes.

Preparation time: 7 minutes
Cooking time: 35 minutes

Preparation time: 4 minutes
Cooking time: 3–4 minutes

crab omelette
kai yat sai poo

75 g/3 oz crab meat

2 eggs

1 heaped teaspoon finely
sliced spring onion greens

¼ onion, chopped

15 g/½ oz coriander leaves,
finely chopped

1 tablespoon fish sauce

4 tablespoons oil

- Combine all the ingredients, except the oil, in a bowl, and stir thoroughly.
- Heat the oil in a wok until it begins to smoke. Empty the contents of the bowl into the wok and turn the heat down to low. The omelette will puff up as it cooks and, after 2–3 minutes, when the underside is brown, turn it over and cook for about another 20 seconds. Fold the omelette in half, slide it on to a plate and serve immediately.

hot and sour fish curry
gang som pla

150 g/5 oz firm, boneless,
white fish, such as haddock
or cod

1 tablespoon Red Curry Paste
(see page 19)

900 ml/1½ pints Fish Stock
(see page 25)

4 baby corn cobs, obliquely
sliced

100 g/3½ oz Chinese leaves,
chopped

2 tablespoons sugar

5 tablespoons fish sauce

40 g/1½ oz tamarind, softened
in 150 ml/¼ pint hot water

- Poach the fish in a pan of gently simmering water for 10–15 minutes, until cooked.
- Lift the fish out of the pan and remove the skin. Put the flesh into a mortar and pound until it is soft and pulpy. Add the curry paste and mix it in well.
- Heat the stock in a saucepan, add the fish paste and bring to the boil, stirring constantly. Reduce the heat and add the baby corn cobs, Chinese leaves, sugar and fish sauce and simmer gently for 10 minutes.
- Stir in the tamarind water, simmer for 5 minutes and serve.

Preparation time: 4 minutes
Cooking time: 30 minutes

Preparation time: 20 minutes
Cooking time: 10 minutes

thai fish cakes
tod mun pla

500 g/1 lb coley fillet, skinned
  and cut into large pieces
1 tablespoon Red Curry Paste
  (see page 19)
1 tablespoon fish sauce
4 lime leaves
25 g/1 oz coriander leaves and
  stalks
2 shallots, chopped
1 stalk lemon grass, sliced
2 garlic cloves, chopped
1 egg
2 teaspoons palm sugar or
  light muscovado sugar
50 g/2 oz broccoli stalk, peeled
  and finely chopped (or finely
  sliced beans or chopped
  water chestnuts)
about 750 ml/1¼ pints oil, for
  deep-frying
coriander sprigs, to garnish
Sweet and Sour Vegetable
  Sauce (see page 117), to serve

- Put the fish, curry paste, fish sauce, lime leaves, coriander, shallots, lemon grass, garlic, egg and sugar into a food processor and blend until smooth. Remove to a bowl and stir in the broccoli.
- Form the mixture into 16 little patties. Heat the oil in a wok, add the patties in batches and deep-fry for about 2–3 minutes, until golden brown all over. Remove from the oil with a bamboo-handled wire basket or a slotted spoon and drain on absorbent kitchen paper.
- Serve the fish cakes hot, garnished with coriander sprigs and with the dipping sauce in a separate bowl.

chilli-fried pomfret

pla lard prik

about 750 ml/1¼ pints oil, for
  deep-frying

1 × 500 g/1 lb pomfret,
  cleaned

6 tomatoes, peeled, deseeded
  and chopped

125 ml/4 fl oz Fish Stock (see
  page 25)

3 garlic cloves, peeled and
  chopped

3 large red chillies, chopped

2 teaspoons palm sugar or
  light muscovado sugar

To garnish:

coriander leaves

spring onion slivers

Crispy Shallots (see page 22)

- Heat the oil in a wok and, while it is heating, make oblique slashes across both sides of the fish.
- Put the fish into the hot oil and deep-fry for about 25 minutes until really crisp, turning once.
- Meanwhile, put the tomatoes, fish stock, garlic, chillies and sugar into another wok or saucepan. Bring to the boil and simmer, stirring occasionally, for about 10–15 minutes until the sauce has thickened and reduced.
- Remove the fish from the oil, drain on kitchen paper and arrange on a plate. Pour over the sauce, garnish and serve.

Preparation time: 10 minutes
Cooking time: 25 minutes

stir-fried squid with basil

pla mook pad grapao

2 tablespoons oil

6 garlic cloves, peeled and
  chopped

12 small green chillies, finely
  sliced

1–2 shallots, chopped

125 g/4 oz squid, cleaned and
  cut into strips

½ green pepper, cored,
  deseeded and chopped

2 tablespoons Fish Stock (see
  page 25)

1 tablespoon fish sauce

1 teaspoon palm sugar or light
  muscovado sugar

15 g/½ oz basil leaves

Crispy Shallots (see page 22),
  to garnish

- Heat the oil in a wok, add the garlic, chillies and shallots and fry for 30 seconds. Add the squid and green pepper, turn the heat to high and stir-fry for 1 minute then reduce the heat and add the stock, fish sauce, sugar and basil. Cook, stirring, for 1 minute, then serve, garnished with the crispy shallots.

Preparation time: 8 minutes
Cooking time: about 3 minutes

prawn vermicelli
gung wun sen

50 g/2 oz pork belly fat

8 tablespoons milk

1 teaspoon dark soy sauce

3 tablespoons oyster sauce

1 teaspoon chopped garlic

5 black peppercorns, crushed

15 g/½ oz coriander leaf, stalk
   and root

20 g/¾ oz julienne ginger

125 g/4 oz bean thread
   vermicelli, soaked

12 raw prawns, shelled, but
   tails left intact

2 tablespoons Fish Stock (see
   page 25), optional

coriander leaves, to garnish

○ Heat the fat in a wok over a moderate heat until the oil runs, stirring occasionally. Remove from the heat and set aside. Discard the fat but leave the oil in the wok.

○ Meanwhile, combine the milk, soy sauce and oyster sauce in a bowl.

○ When the oil has cooled down a bit – about 5 minutes – add the garlic, peppercorns, coriander and ginger and stir-fry for 30 seconds. Add the vermicelli and milk mixture, stir together thoroughly over a high heat, then reduce the heat to low, cover the wok and cook for 12 minutes.

○ Finally, turn the heat up, add the prawns and the fish stock, if the sauce looks too thick, and cook, stirring, for about 2–3 minutes, until all the prawns have turned pink.

○ Turn into a serving bowl and garnish with coriander leaves.

1 tablespoon oil

50 g/2 oz onion, finely sliced

1 tablespoon minced garlic

1 tablespoon ground black
   pepper

50 g/2 oz broccoli stem,
   peeled and sliced

25 g/1 oz oyster mushrooms,
   torn

12 raw prawns, shelled

1 teaspoon sugar

4–6 tablespoons Fish Stock
   (see page 25)

4 tablespoons light soy sauce

15 g/½ oz chopped coriander
   leaves, to garnish

stir-fried prawns with garlic
gung pad kratiem

○ Heat the oil in a wok, add the onion, garlic and pepper and stir-fry for 30 seconds. Add the broccoli stem and stir-fry for 1 minute. Add the mushrooms and stir-fry for 30 seconds then add the prawns, sugar, 4 tablespoons of the stock and the soy sauce. Stir-fry over a high heat for 1–2 minutes, adding more fish stock if the dish is drying out.

○ Serve immediately, garnished with coriander leaves.

Preparation time: 15 minutes
Cooking time: 5 minutes

Thai people have a great love of beauty as well as food, and they often make their salads and vegetables into little works of art. Chillies and spring onions are turned into leaves and tassels, root vegetables into flowers or fish. Even if you are not a fruit or vegetable carver, you can make your salads beautiful. They should always be served on a plate rather than in a bowl so that the effort that has gone into arranging them prettily can be fully appreciated. Although the following recipes are quite specific, it is fun trying different combinations and you can add extra ingredients too, such as thinly sliced green beans, mustard and cress, lightly cooked asparagus, grated cucumber, blanched bean sprouts and fresh herbs.

salads and *vegetables*

duck salad
yam pet

¼ roast duck
6 small green chillies, finely
   sliced
½ red onion, finely sliced
25 g/1 oz coriander leaf, stalk
   and root, finely chopped
½ tomato, cut into quarters
juice of 2 limes
1 heaped teaspoon palm sugar
   or light muscovado sugar
1½ tablespoons fish sauce

To serve:
lettuce leaves
mint leaves

- Take the skin and meat off the duck and cut into small pieces.
- Heat a wok and then turn the heat off. Put the duck into the wok to warm it through and then add all the remaining ingredients, stirring and turning them thoroughly for 3 minutes.
- To serve, arrange the lettuce leaves and mint on one side of a serving dish and place the duck salad beside them.

watercress in garlic and oyster sauce
pad pak nam mon hoi

- Heat the oil in a wok, add the garlic and stir-fry until golden.
- Add the watercress and stir-fry for 30 seconds then add the oyster sauce and stock. Continue to stir-fry vigorously for 1 minute then serve.

Preparation time: 2 minutes
Cooking time: 5 minutes

2 tablespoons oil
6 garlic cloves, finely chopped
300 g/10 oz watercress
1 tablespoon oyster sauce
2 tablespoons Vegetable Stock
   (see page 24)

salted egg salad

yam kai kem

10 small green and red chillies,
  finely sliced

¾ onion, sliced

20 g/¾ oz coriander leaf, stalk
  and root, chopped

15 g/½ oz spring onion,
  obliquely sliced

3 tablespoons lime juice

1 teaspoon fish sauce

1 teaspoon palm sugar or light
  muscovado sugar

3 Salted Eggs (see page 112),
  shelled and quartered

- Place all of the ingredients except for the eggs in a bowl and mix thoroughly for 2–3 minutes.
- Arrange the sauce on a serving dish. Add the egg quarters, turn once carefully to coat in the sauce, and serve.

Preparation time: 4 minutes

Preparation time: 15 minutes
Cooking time: 45 minutes

minced fish salad
yam pla duk foo

1 x 625 g/1¼ lb catfish, cleaned
12 small green chillies, finely
  sliced
½ red onion, finely sliced
15 g/½ oz coriander leaf, stalk
  and root, finely chopped
3 tablespoons lime juice
3 tablespoons fish sauce
1½ tablespoons palm sugar or
  light muscovado sugar
¼ green mango, grated
  (optional)
40 g/1½ oz Crushed Roasted
  Nuts (see page 24)
about 750 ml/1¼ pints oil, for
  deep-frying

To garnish:
shredded white cabbage
coriander leaves
fresh chillies

- Place the catfish under a preheated grill and cook for 30 minutes, turning once, or until cooked and soft. Set aside to cool.
- Skin the fish and take off the flesh, carefully removing any bones. Mince the fish in a food processor or chop it very finely.
- Put all the remaining ingredients into a bowl and mix well.
- Heat the oil in a wok until hot enough for deep-frying, then add some of the minced fish. Cook each batch of minced fish for 4–5 minutes, stirring occasionally. Remove with a slotted spoon and drain on kitchen paper.
- To serve, arrange the minced fish on a serving dish. Pour the sauce over the top of the fish and garnish it with fresh shredded cabbage, coriander leaves and chillies.

stir-fried leaf vegetables *pad pak*

2 tablespoons oil
325 g/11 oz torn mixed green
  vegetables, such as spinach,
  Chinese leaves, lettuce,
  watercress
2 tablespoons oyster sauce
1 teaspoon palm sugar or light
  muscovado sugar
2 tablespoons Vegetable Stock
  (see page 24)
2 teaspoons Garlic Oil (see
  page 22)

- Heat the oil in a wok, toss in the vegetables and stir-fry for 30 seconds. Add the oyster sauce, sugar and stock and cook for about 3 minutes, stirring all the time, until the leaves have wilted.
- Turn on to a serving dish and sprinkle the garlic oil on the top.

Preparation time: 5 minutes
Cooking time: 5 minutes

Preparation time: 10–15 minutes
Cooking time: 3–4 minutes

deep-fried dried fish salad *yam pla krob*

- Pound the chillies and red onion in a mortar. Add the coriander and pound again. Add the lime juice, fish sauce, sugar and green mango and pound once more until the ingredients are thoroughly mixed.
- Heat the oil in a wok and, when it is hot, throw in the little dried fish and cook them for 2–3 minutes until golden and crispy. Remove the fish and drain on kitchen paper.
- Arrange some lettuce leaves on a serving dish and place the fish on top. Pour over the sauce from the mortar and serve.

6 small green chillies, finely
  sliced
½ red onion, finely chopped
15 g/½ oz coriander leaf, stalk
  and root, finely chopped
2 tablespoons lime juice
½ tablespoon fish sauce
1½ tablespoons sugar
¼ green mango, grated
about 750 ml/1¼ pints oil, for
  deep-frying
50 g/2 oz small dried fish
lettuce leaves, to serve

Preparation time: 8 minutes
Cooking time: 1–2 minutes

squid salad
yam pla mook

½ red onion, sliced

1 tomato, cut into 8 pieces

5 g/¼ oz coriander leaves,
  roughly chopped

5 small green or red chillies,
  finely sliced

125 g/4 oz squid, sliced

3 tablespoons lime juice

2 teaspoons palm sugar or
  light muscovado sugar

3 tablespoons fish sauce

15 g/½ oz shredded carrot

15 g/½ oz shredded white
  cabbage

- Place the onion, tomato, coriander and chillies together in a mixing bowl.
- Put the squid briefly in a saucepan of boiling water and cook for about 1½ minutes. Remove from the pan and combine with the onion and tomato mixture.
- Add the lime juice, sugar and fish sauce and mix well together for 1–2 minutes.
- Finally add the carrot and cabbage, give the salad a quick stir, turn it all into a bowl and serve.

Preparation time: 10 minutes
Cooking time: 7 minutes

warm chicken salad
laab gai

1 tablespoon oil

150 g/5 oz boneless, skinless
  chicken breast, cut into
  bite-sized pieces

1 tablespoon Chicken Stock
  (see page 25)

1 teaspoon palm sugar or light
  muscovado sugar

2 tablespoons fish sauce

2 teaspoons Ground Roast
  Rice (see page 21)

1 stalk lemon grass, finely
  sliced

5 lime leaves, finely shredded

½ red onion, sliced

1 teaspoon dried chillies

15 g/½ oz coriander leaves

mint sprigs, to garnish

- Heat the oil in a wok, add the chicken and stir-fry over a high heat for about 4 minutes until cooked through.
- Add the stock and cook, stirring constantly, for 1 minute.
- Transfer the chicken to a bowl, stir in all the remaining ingredients and mix thoroughly for 1–2 minutes. Serve, garnished with mint sprigs.

Preparation time: 5 minutes

thai steak tartare
laab isaan

150 g/5 oz steak tartare

1 teaspoon palm sugar or light
muscovado sugar

2 tablespoons fish sauce

2 teaspoons Ground Roast
Rice (see page 21)

1 stalk lemon grass, finely
sliced

5 lime leaves, finely shredded

1 shallot, finely chopped

1 teaspoon dried red chillies

15 g/½ oz coriander leaves

mint sprigs, to garnish

To serve:

lettuce

tomatoes, quartered

cucumber chunks

Steak tartare is very high quality minced beef: rump steak, or fillet of course, would be ideal. Tell your butcher that you are going to make steak tartare and ask him to mince the beef finely.

- Put all the ingredients into a bowl and stir together thoroughly for 2–3 minutes.
- Place the lettuce leaves on a serving dish and spoon the steak on to them. Arrange the mint sprigs on one side and the tomato and cucumber on the other.

Variation: thai fried steak tartare

- Heat 1 tablespoon of oil in a wok, add the steak and stir-fry over a high heat for 3 minutes. Add 1 tablespoon of chicken stock and continue cooking, stirring constantly, for 1 minute. Transfer the mince to a bowl, add all the remaining ingredients, mix thoroughly for 2–3 minutes and serve as for the main recipe.

Rice is the staple food of Thailand and is celebrated as such. In the spring the Ploughing Ceremony is held on the large open space by the Grand Palace in Bangkok in the presence of the King. This colourful ceremony, that predates the arrival of Buddhism in Thailand, is to please the gods and thereby ensure a good harvest. Rice freezes very well and can be a brilliant stand-by if you find you suddenly have unexpected guests. Fried rice should be made with cold cooked rice because the oil in which it is cooked will coat the cold grains but would be absorbed by warm grains. Noodles probably came to Thailand from China but are now totally assimilated into Thai cuisine. They are the only food that Thais use chopsticks to eat.

rice and *noodles*

Preparation time: 10 minutes
Cooking time: 6–7 minutes

fried noodles with chicken and broccoli
pad kwetio sy gai

1½ tablespoons oil

1 large garlic clove, peeled and chopped

¼ onion, chopped

125 g/4 oz skinless, boneless chicken breast, chopped

1 egg

150 g/5 oz rice noodles, soaked

1½ tablespoons palm sugar or light muscovado sugar

1 tablespoon tamarind water or distilled white vinegar

5 tablespoons light soy sauce

75 g/3 oz broccoli floret and stalk

1 tablespoon chopped red pepper

75 g/3 oz chopped spring onion – greens and bulb

50 g/2 oz bean sprouts

2 tablespoons Crushed Roasted Nuts (see page 24)

½ teaspoon ground black pepper

coriander leaves, to garnish

- Heat the oil in a wok, add the garlic, onion and chopped chicken and stir-fry over a high heat for 1 minute.
- Lower the heat and break the egg into the mixture, stirring constantly. Add the noodles, sugar, tamarind water, soy sauce and broccoli and cook, stirring, for 2 minutes.
- Add the remaining ingredients, turn the heat up and stir-fry vigorously for about 1 minute then turn it all out on to a serving dish. Garnish with coriander leaves.

fried rice *kao pad*

4 tablespoons oil

1 egg

375 g/12 oz cold cooked rice

1 teaspoon sugar

2 tablespoons fish sauce

50 g/2 oz cabbage, roughly chopped

pinch of black pepper

- Heat the oil in a wok then break the egg into it, stirring it around and breaking it up.
- Add the rice and mix well for 2–3 minutes or until all the rice is separated. Add the sugar, fish sauce, cabbage and black pepper and stir-fry vigorously for 3–4 minutes, until the cabbage has wilted. Serve at once.

Preparation time: 1 minute
Cooking time: 8 minutes

Preparation time: 6 minutes
Cooking time: 10 minutes

fried rice with pork and mushrooms

kao pad muu gup het

3 tablespoons oil

100 g/3½ oz pork, cut into
  bite-sized pieces

1 garlic clove, peeled and
  chopped

1 egg

375 g/12 oz cold cooked rice

1 tomato, cut into 8 pieces

1 teaspoon palm sugar or light
  muscovado sugar

3 tablespoons fish sauce

65 g/2½ oz oyster mushrooms,
  sliced

15 g/½ oz spring onion,
  obliquely sliced

coriander leaves, to garnish

○ Heat the oil in a wok, add the pork and garlic and stir-fry for 2–3 minutes until they begin to turn golden. Break the egg into the wok and stir it around well. Add the rice and stir-fry for 2–3 minutes then add the tomato and sugar and stir-fry for 1 minute. Add the fish sauce and stir, then add the mushrooms and stir-fry for 1 minute. Finally add the spring onion and mix it all together thoroughly.

○ Turn the rice into a bowl and serve, garnished with the coriander leaves.

drunkard's noodles
pad ki mao

20 small green and red chillies

9 garlic cloves

3 tablespoons oil

125 g/4 oz minced pork

400 g/13 oz fresh Ho Fun
noodles

2 tablespoons palm sugar or
light muscovado sugar

4 tablespoons light soy sauce

1 tablespoon dark soy sauce

1 tablespoon yellow beans

1 tablespoon oyster sauce

75 g/3 oz Chinese leaves,
chopped

15 g/½ oz basil leaves

- Pound the chillies with the garlic in a mortar for about 3 minutes until well broken down.
- Heat the oil in a wok, add the chillies and garlic, and stir-fry for 1 minute. Add the pork and stir-fry over a high heat for about 5 minutes.
- Add the noodles, sugar, light and dark soy sauce, yellow beans, oyster sauce and Chinese leaves and stir-fry for 1 minute, mixing the noodles well with the other ingredients. Finally, add the basil leaves. Give it all a good stir and transfer to a serving dish.

Preparation time: 4–5 minutes
Cooking time: 8 minutes

noodles with gravy
kwetio lard nar gung

1 tablespoon oil

400 g/13 oz fresh Ho Fun
noodles

1 tablespoon dark soy sauce

Gravy:

2 tablespoons oil

250 g/8 oz mixed green
vegetables, such as broccoli,
curly cabbage, sugar snap
peas or Chinese leaves

1 tablespoon oyster sauce

1 tablespoon yellow beans

2 tablespoons palm sugar or
light muscovado sugar

600 ml/1 pint Vegetable Stock
(see page 24)

100 ml/3½ fl oz light soy sauce

8–12 raw prawns, shelled, but
tails left intact

1 tablespoon Crispy Garlic
(see page 22)

1 teaspoon cornflour

- Heat 1 tablespoon of oil in a saucepan, add the noodles and the dark soy sauce and stir them around for 1 minute. Remove from the heat and reserve.
- Make the gravy: heat the oil in a wok and throw in the vegetables, oyster sauce, yellow beans and sugar and stir-fry for 1 minute then add the stock and light soy sauce. Keep on stirring the boiling liquid and add the prawns, which will turn pink in 1–2 minutes. Add the crispy garlic.
- In a small bowl mix the cornflour with a little water and add it to the wok to thicken the gravy.
- To serve, turn the noodles on to a plate and ladle the gravy over them.

Preparation time: 12 minutes
Cooking time: 10 minutes

shrimp paste rice with chicken
kao kuk gabi

In Thailand, this dish is usually served with a bowl of Pork Ball and Black Fungus Soup (see page 43).

625 g/1¼ lb cold cooked rice

2 tablespoons oil

200 g/7 oz chicken, skinned and cut into bite-sized pieces

2½ tablespoons palm sugar or light muscovado sugar

3 tablespoons light soy sauce

2 tablespoons dark soy sauce

2 tablespoons Chicken Stock (see page 25)

20 g/¾ oz shrimp paste

½ red onion, sliced

1 courgette, obliquely sliced

1 lime, quartered

Thai Egg Strips (see page 32), to serve

- Reheat the rice in a steamer.
- Meanwhile, heat the oil in a wok, add the chicken and stir-fry for 2 minutes or until all the pieces have turned white. Add the sugar and the light and dark soy sauces, stir well and cook for another 1 minute then add the stock and turn the heat off.
- Put the hot rice into a bowl and stir in the shrimp paste thoroughly, so the rice begins to look a browny colour.
- Pile the rice on to serving plates and arrange some red onion, courgette and lime around the edge of each one. Reheat the chicken for 30 seconds then pile it on to the rice. Put the egg strips on top of the chicken or serve them separately.

Preparation time: 7 minutes
Cooking time: 10 minutes

Preparation time: 3 minutes
Cooking time: 15–20 minutes

red pork rice
kao muu daeng

Traditionally, in Thailand, Red Pork Rice would be eaten with Pork Ball and Tofu Soup (see page 47).

250 g/8 oz Red Roast Pork (see page 58)
375 g/12 oz rice
1–2 tablespoons Chicken Stock (see page 25)
coriander sprigs, to garnish

- Cut the cooked pork into slices. Cook the rice in the normal way (see page 20).
- Put the chicken stock into the roasting tin, in which you cooked the pork and heat, stirring, to de-glaze.
- To serve, place the rice on a serving plate, arrange the pork on top and pour over the juices from the roasting tin. Garnish with coriander sprigs.

crispy noodles
mee krob

40 g/1½ oz tamarind pod, soaked and squeezed into 300 ml/½ pint hot water
200 g/7 oz palm sugar or light muscovado sugar
75 ml/3 fl oz tomato ketchup
3 tablespoons fish sauce
about 750 ml/1¼ pints oil, for deep-frying
125 g/4 oz rice vermicelli
40 g/1½ oz ready-fried tofu cut into 2.5 cm x 5 mm/ 1 inch x ¼ inch pieces
spring onion tops, sliced, to garnish

- Heat the tamarind water in a wok and melt the sugar in it – it will foam up. Add the ketchup and stir for 1 minute then add the fish sauce. Cook, stirring, for 20–25 minutes – the sauce will gradually thicken until it is almost the consistency of jam and will stick to the noodles. Remove it from the heat and allow it to cool down somewhat.
- In another wok, heat the oil until it is hot enough to deep-fry the noodles and then drop them in, a handful at a time. They will puff up and expand immediately; remove them with a slotted spoon on to kitchen paper, to drain.
- When all the noodles are fried, put them into a large bowl and drizzle the sweet red sauce over them, working it in carefully with your hands until the crispy white noodles turn a pinky-brown. Pour off all but 1 tablespoon of the oil from the wok and reserve it for another time. Arrange the noodles on a serving dish.
- Quickly fry the tofu pieces in the wok, then arrange them on top of the noodles. Sprinkle with the sliced spring onion tops.

Preparation time: 6 minutes
Cooking time: 35 minutes

From left: pickled ginger; pickled garlic (page 110–111)

sauces
and *pickles*

Pickled vegetables are often served as a side dish with a meal and some are used during cooking. They are another example of the Thais' love of contrasting tastes and textures. Dipping sauces perform the same function, and some form of chilli-hot sauce will be on the table at every meal. Spring rolls, fritters, fried fish and raw vegetables are all served with different sauces to accompany them – sweet and hot or sour and hot, depending on your taste. *Nam Prik* – literally chilli water – is the basic hot sauce, but when it is combined with pork it makes a wonderful kind of Thai spaghetti sauce. Not only is it good as a dipping sauce for raw vegetables but it is delicious with rice or noodles too.

Preparation time: 30 minutes, plus standing
Cooking time: 10 minutes

pickled garlic
kratiem dong

6 garlic bulbs
1.2 litres/2 pints water
300 ml/½ pint distilled
   white vinegar
50 g/2 oz granulated sugar
1 tablespoon salt

- Separate all the garlic cloves and peel them.
- Bring the water, vinegar, sugar and salt to the boil in a saucepan, then reduce the heat and simmer for 5 minutes.
- Add the garlic to the pan, return to the boil and boil hard for 1 minute.
- Remove the saucepan from the heat, allow the garlic mixture to cool then transfer it into airtight containers and store in the refrigerator. Leave for 10 days before eating.

Preparation time: 2 minutes
Cooking time: 4 minutes

fresh cucumber pickle *dong tangkwa*

1 large cucumber, peeled
1 shallot, thinly sliced
75 ml/3 fl oz water
2 tablespoons granulated sugar
2½ tablespoons distilled white
   vinegar
pinch of dried red chilli
pinch of salt

- Cut the cucumber in half lengthways and slice the halves into 5 mm/¼ inch thick slices. Put the cucumber and shallot in a bowl and set aside.
- Heat the water in a saucepan, add the sugar and stir until dissolved. Remove the pan from the heat and allow it to cool a little then add the vinegar, chilli and salt. Pour the pickle mixture over the cucumber and shallot and give it all a good stir. Cover the bowl and put it into the refrigerator until you are ready to serve. This fresh pickle will last for 4–5 days in an airtight container in the refrigerator.

Preparation time: 40 minutes, plus standing
Cooking time: 18–20 minutes

pickled ginger

125 g/4 oz fresh root ginger
¼ teaspoon salt
125 ml/4 fl oz rice vinegar
1 tablespoon caster sugar

- Peel the ginger and cut it into the thinnest possible slices. Leave it to stand in a bowl of cold water for 30 minutes.
- Boil a saucepan of water. Remove the ginger from the bowl of cold water with a slotted spoon and drop it into the boiling water. Bring back to a brisk boil over a high heat, drain and allow to cool.
- Spread out the ginger on a plate and sprinkle with salt. In a small saucepan, combine the vinegar and sugar and heat until the sugar has fully dissolved. Place the ginger in a jar and pour the mixture over it, mixing thoroughly. Allow to cool, then put the top on the jar and place it in the refrigerator.
- The pickled ginger will turn a very pale pink colour, and will be ready to use after 1 week. It will keep in the refrigerator for 3–4 months.

Preparation time: 25 minutes, plus cooling and standing
Cooking time: 15 minutes

rice water pickle

2.4 litres/4 pints water

250 g/8 oz glutinous rice

1 mooli radish

2 carrots

375 g/12 oz Chinese leaves or
cabbage

3 garlic cloves, thinly sliced

1 tablespoon peeled and thinly
sliced fresh root ginger

1 teaspoon black peppercorns

2 tablespoons salt

1 shallot, peeled

2 large fresh chillies (preferably
red and yellow)

- Bring the water to the boil in a large saucepan, add the rice and boil for 15 minutes. Meanwhile, peel the mooli and carrots and slice them thinly, and cut the Chinese leaves into 2.5 cm/1 inch slices. Pat the vegetables dry with kitchen paper and set aside.
- Strain the water off the rice into a bowl, then set the water aside to cool. Discard the rice.
- Take a 2.4 litre/4 pint jar and fill it with layers of vegetables, sprinkling garlic, ginger, peppercorns and salt between each layer and ending with a sprinkling of salt on top. Bury the whole shallot and the whole chillies in the middle.
- Add the cooled rice water to just cover the top layer, cover the jar with muslin and let it stand in a cool place for 4 days, making sure the level of the liquid does not drop. If it does, top it up with cold water.
- The pickle will be ready to eat after 4 days; you can put the lid on the jar and keep it in the refrigerator, where the pickle will keep for several weeks.

salted eggs
kai kem

1.2 litres/2 pints water

125 g/4 oz salt

4 eggs, in their shells

- Heat the water in a saucepan and dissolve the salt in it. Remove from the heat and allow to cool.
- When the water is cool, pour it into a jar and gently add the whole eggs. Put the lid on and allow to stand at room temperature for 15 days.
- Remove the eggs from the jar and hard-boil.

Preparation time: 10 minutes, plus cooling and standing
Cooking time: 10 minutes

soy and vinegar dipping sauce

3 tablespoons distilled white
    vinegar or Chinese rice
    vinegar
3 tablespoons dark soy sauce
1½ teaspoons caster sugar
2 small fresh red chillies,
    finely sliced

◉ Combine all the ingredients in a bowl and stir until the sugar has dissolved.

Preparation time: 2 minutes

plum sauce

5 tablespoons distilled white
    vinegar or Chinese rice
    vinegar
4 tablespoons plum jam
1 small fresh red chilli, finely
    sliced

◉ Put the vinegar and jam in a small saucepan and heat gently, mixing thoroughly. Remove from the heat, turn into a small bowl and allow to cool.
◉ Add the sliced fresh chilli before serving.

Preparation time: 1 minute
Cooking time: 2 minutes

Preparation time: 4–5 minutes

lime and fish sauce
nam prik num bar

6 tablespoons lime juice

2 teaspoons palm sugar or
  light muscovado sugar

½–1 teaspoon fish sauce

½ teaspoon finely chopped
  shallot

1 teaspoon finely chopped
  red chilli

◉ Squeeze the lime juice into a small bowl and add the sugar. Mix well until the sugar dissolves. Add the remaining ingredients and serve.

hot sweet sauce

100 ml/3 1/2 fl oz distilled
  white vinegar or Chinese rice
  vinegar

60 g/2½ oz palm sugar or light
  muscovado sugar

¼ teaspoon salt

1 small fresh green chilli, finely
  chopped

1 small fresh red chilli, finely
  chopped

◉ Pour the vinegar into a small saucepan and place over a gentle heat. Add the sugar and salt and cook, stirring, until the sugar has dissolved. Remove from the heat and allow to cool.

◉ Pour the sauce into a small bowl and add the chopped fresh chillies.

Preparation time: 1 minute
Cooking time: 1–2 minutes

Preparation time: 3–6 minutes
Cooking time: 1½ hours

sweet sauce
saus nam tam

½ red pepper, with its seeds
125 g/4 oz pineapple, fresh or
 tinned
150 ml/¼ pint pineapple juice
1.2 litres/2 pints water
300 ml/½ pint distilled white
 vinegar
400 g/13 oz granulated sugar

◉ Blend the red pepper, pineapple and pineapple juice together in a food processor and pour it into a wok or saucepan. Add the water, vinegar and sugar, give it a good stir and cook, simmering, for 1½ hours, until the sauce has reduced and thickened.

◉ The amount of sauce this makes will give you enough for your immediate use, and you can store the rest in an airtight container, at room temperature or in the refrigerator, for about 10 days.

easy sweet and sour sauce
nam gym

◉ Put all the ingredients into a saucepan or wok and bring to the boil, stirring. Reduce the heat and cook, simmering, for 20 minutes, stirring occasionally.

Cooking time: 25 minutes

750 ml/1¼ pints pineapple
 juice
4 tablespoons tomato ketchup
1 tablespoon tomato purée
5 tablespoons sugar
7 tablespoons distilled white
 vinegar

Preparation time: 5 minutes, plus cooling
Cooking time: 5 minutes

sweet and sour vegetable sauce

50 ml/2 fl oz distilled white
  vinegar
125 g/4 oz sugar
1½ tablespoons water
2 teaspoons fish sauce
50 g/2 oz cucumber, finely
  diced
50 g/2 oz carrot, finely diced
1 shallot, finely chopped
2 small red or green chillies,
  finely sliced

- Put the vinegar, sugar and water into a small saucepan and heat gently, until the sugar dissolves. Bring to the boil and boil for 1 minute, then set the saucepan to one side and allow the liquid to cool.
- Stir the fish sauce, cucumber, carrot, shallot and chillies into the cooled sauce, pour into a small bowl and serve.

easy satay sauce
nam gym satay

1 tablespoon oil
2 teaspoons Red Curry Paste
  (see page 19)
3 tablespoons coconut milk
125 ml/4 fl oz water
3 tablespoons palm sugar or
  light muscovado sugar
125 g/4 oz peanuts, crushed

- Heat the oil in a wok, add the curry paste and cook for 30 seconds then add all the remaining ingredients. Stir well and leave to cook over a low heat for 10–15 minutes, stirring occasionally. Add a little more water if you feel the sauce is becoming too thick. To serve, turn the sauce into a small bowl.

Preparation time: 1 minute
Cooking time: 15–17 minutes

There are many different kinds of sweet things available in Thailand, but the usual way to finish a meal is with a large plate of mixed fruits. In the main, the more complicated and time-consuming recipes are only cooked for special occasions. Many of the little cakes and sweetmeats can be bought from the market, as can mangoes and sticky rice, during the season. I have suggested simple recipes for the most part, but again, you can experiment with them. Try sliced banana or whole lychees in the coconut cream custard, or use black glutinous rice, instead of white rice, with mangoes. Make pancakes using coconut milk instead of cow's milk and rice flour instead of wheat flour; roll them up around fresh fruit and sprinkle them with palm sugar and toasted flaked coconut.

Clockwise from left: jack-fruit seeds; limeade; and coconut cream custard (pages 120-121)

desserts

Preparation time: 5 minutes
Cooking time: 15–20 minutes

coconut cream custard

sang kia maprow on

2 large eggs
200 ml/7 fl oz coconut milk
175 g/6 oz palm sugar or light
  muscovado sugar
¼ teaspoon salt
2 banana leaves (optional)

- Beat the eggs together in a bowl and add the coconut milk and sugar. Mix well, add the salt and mix again.
- Pour this mixture into 4 ramekins or, if you prefer, into banana leaf bowls.
- To make banana leaf bowls, cut 8 equal-size circles from the banana leaves and place 2 pieces together, shiny side out. Make 4 pleats opposite each other, and secure with toothpicks to form a bowl. Make 3 more bowls in the same way.
- Put the filled ramekins or banana leaf bowls into a steamer and steam for 15–20 minutes. Serve warm, on a plate.

limeade

nam manao

If you roll the limes around quite hard on a board with your hand, you will find that you get more juice from them.

6 limes
125 g/4 oz caster sugar
750 ml/1¼ pints boiling water
pinch of salt
ice cubes
mint sprigs, to decorate

- Halve and squeeze the limes into a large jug then put the squeezed halves into a heat-proof jug with the sugar and boiling water. Leave to infuse for 15 minutes.
- Add the salt, give the infusion a good stir then strain it into the jug with the lime juice. Add half a dozen ice cubes, cover and refrigerate for 2 hours or until cold.
- To serve, place 3–4 ice cubes in each glass and pour the limeade over them. Decorate with a sprig of mint.

Makes 1.2 litres/2 pints
Preparation time: 6 minutes, plus infusing and chilling

Makes about 20
Preparation time: 5 minutes, plus soaking and cooling
Cooking time: about 30 minutes

jack-fruit seeds
met kanun

○ Put the beans, coconut milk and palm sugar into a wok over a very low heat and stir and mash constantly until the mixture comes together and becomes thick and pliable like a dough mixture. You must keep stirring and turning all the time as the mixture burns very easily. When it has reached the correct consistency, remove it from the wok and set aside to cool.

○ Put the water and caster sugar into a wok or saucepan and boil until it becomes thick enough to make a glaze.

○ Form oblong shapes about 3–5 cm/1½–2 inches long from the cooling mixture – they are said to resemble jack-fruit seeds – and coat each one in the egg yolk then carefully put them into the simmering sugar glaze, in batches. Roll them around in the glaze for 2 minutes, then remove with a slotted spoon and arrange on a serving dish. Make sure they do not touch each other or they will stick together.

125 g/4 oz split yellow beans, soaked for at least 3 hours
400 ml/14 fl oz can coconut milk
125 g/4 oz palm sugar or light muscovado sugar
300 ml/½ pint water
200 g/7 oz caster sugar
3–4 egg yolks, whisked

Preparation time: 2–3 minutes
Cooking time: 40 minutes

tapioca and young coconut
beeak sar koo maprow on

125 g/4 oz tapioca pearls

400 g/13 oz can of young coconut flesh or 175 g/6 oz fresh young coconut flesh

4 tablespoons thick coconut milk

1 teaspoon palm sugar or light muscovado sugar

pinch of salt

- Put the tapioca pearls into 1.2 litres/2 pints of water and boil for 10 minutes. Drain the tapioca, cover with fresh water and boil gently for about 30 minutes until it is cooked, occasionally topping up the liquid.
- Turn off the heat and add the young coconut flesh, in pieces, and its juice.
- Mix together the coconut milk, sugar and salt in a small bowl.
- Serve the dessert warm with a tablespoon of the coconut milk mixture on each portion.

mango and sticky rice
kaoniao mamuang

500 g/1 lb glutinous rice, soaked for at least 6 hours or overnight

150 g/5 oz sugar

300 ml/½ pint coconut milk

2 ripe mangoes

- Drain and rinse the rice well. Cook in a steamer for about 30 minutes. Give the rice a good shake halfway through steaming to ensure it is evenly cooked.
- While the rice is steaming, combine the sugar and coconut milk in a large bowl and stir well.
- When the rice is cooked, transfer it to the coconut mixture and stir thoroughly for 2–3 minutes to achieve a rather creamy consistency. Cover with a lid and allow to stand at room temperature for 30 minutes.
- Before serving, slice the mangoes and arrange them attractively on a dish around the rice.

Preparation time: 10 minutes, plus soaking and standing
Cooking time: 30 minutes

Preparation time: 15–20 minutes

fresh fruit platter

◉ Peel and thickly slice the mangoes and cut the papaya into four or eight pieces. Peel the lychees. Cut the watermelon into chunks, removing as many of the seeds as you can.

◉ Arrange the fruit on a serving plate, with the lime quarters ready to squeeze over the papaya.

2 ripe mangoes

1 small ripe papaya

250 g/8 oz lychees

1 slice watermelon

1 lime, cut into quarters

Preparation time: 2 minutes
Cooking time: 10 minutes

bananas in coconut milk

This is a very easy and un-fussy pudding. It doesn't look particularly appealing but it tastes really good.

200 ml/7 fl oz coconut milk

100 ml/3½ fl oz water

3 tablespoons palm sugar or light muscovado sugar

1 large or 2 small bananas, halved lengthways and each half cut into 4 pieces

◉ Put the coconut milk, water and sugar into a saucepan and simmer, stirring occasionally, for about 6 minutes. Add the bananas and cook for 4 minutes until heated through.

Preparation time: 5 minutes
Cooking time: 15 minutes

thai fried bananas
gluay buat chea

150 g/5 oz self-raising flour

125 ml/4 fl oz water

2 teaspoons palm sugar or light muscovado sugar

1 tablespoon toasted sesame seeds

about 750 ml/1¼ pints oil, for deep-frying

4 bananas

3 tablespoons toasted desiccated coconut

◉ Mix the flour, water, sugar and sesame seeds in a bowl to make a light batter.
◉ Heat the oil in a wok and, while it is heating, peel the bananas. Cut them in half lengthways, and cut each half into 2–3 pieces. Coat the bananas thoroughly in the batter. When the oil is hot enough, carefully slide in the banana in 2 batches for 5–7 minutes and fry until golden brown. Remove and drain on kitchen paper.
◉ To serve, arrange the banana fritters on a serving plate and sprinkle with the toasted coconut.

index